Free Radio

Critical Studies in Communication and in the Cultural Industries

Herbert I. Schiller, Series Editor

FREE RADIO

Electronic Civil Disobedience

LAWRENCE SOLEY

Foreword by
Louis N. Hiken

Westview Press
A Member of the Perseus Books Group

Critical Studies in Communication and in the Cultural Industries

Copyright © 1999 by Westview Press, A Member of Perseus Books, L.L.C.

Published in 1999 in the United States of America by Westview Press, 5500 Central Avenue, Boulder,
Colorado 80301-2877, and in the United Kingdom by Westview Press, 12 Hid's Copse Road, Cumnor
Hill, Oxford OX2 9JJ

Library of Congress Cataloging-in-Publication Data
Soley, Lawrence C.
   Free radio: electronic civil disobedience / Lawrence Soley.
      p.   cm. — (Critical studies in communication and in the
cultural industries)
   Includes bibliographical references and index.
   ISBN 0-8133-9064-8
   1. Pirate radio broadcsting—United States.   2. Radio
broadcasting policy—United States.   I. Title.   II. Series.
HE8697.65.U6S65   1999
384.54—dc21   98-29489
                                                                                      CIP

The paper used in this publication meets the requirements of the American National Standard for
Permanence of Paper for Printed Library Materials Z39.48-1984.

10   9   8   7   6   5   4   3   2   1

Contents

Foreword

In 1993, I attended a meeting at the home of Jesse Drew, one of the producer-directors active with Paper Tiger Television. His guest that evening was Japanese engineer and activist, Tetsuo Kogawa. Mr. Kogawa was an outspoken advocate of microradio as a two-way system of communication. He felt that a microradio station should be no more powerful than was necessary to reach people within bicycle range of the transmitter. "In that way," he explained, "you can be assured of community participation in whatever is being broadcast over the air. If people feel that they are not interested in what is being broadcast, they don't have to participate in the dialogue. But if they do have an opinion, they can bicycle over to the station and express it in a timely way."

While he was giving his talk about the social and political uses of microradio technology, he was simultaneously soldering and scotch-taping a series of Radio Shack parts, worth about fifteen dollars, to a paper plate. Within fifteen minutes, he had completed his soldering and announced that he had finished "building" his transmitter. He asked if someone had a little handheld tape recorder and a cable TV antenna. He also requested that somebody turn on the FM radio so that he could "adjust the frequency." Within three more minutes, he announced that we were "on the air."

His stunned audience sat in silence. The room was filled with media activists—not a notoriously silent group of individuals. As I look back at it, I would have thought that we would all have jumped at the chance to wax eloquent about some subject dear to our hearts. Instead, we sat there speechless. When confronted with the actual power and ability to communicate with our neighbors in San Francisco's Mission District, we were immobilized.

Within seconds, Jesse's teenage daughter quietly picked up the tape recorder and began talking to her neighbors about what was happening in the community. She started out with the statement: "Yo, Mission District, this is Free Radio San Francisco, talking to you live." Her words were eloquent and unfiltered. The adults stared at each other amused and astonished by the contradiction. We adults were trying to figure out how to sound like some left-wing equivalent to Walter Cronkite, and were, of course, silenced at the prospect. This teenager was the only person in the room who was so unintimidated by the "new" medium as to be able to talk spontaneously over the air.

Some of us got in our cars to drive around the area and see how far the transmissions went. Upon returning to the house, we estimated that the broadcasts covered the area of about one precinct. Not bad for a city about to have an election in two weeks.

For weeks after that meeting, I had discussions with others who had been there as to why none of us felt comfortable picking up the "microphone" and talking about the issues that were important to us. It surely wasn't because we didn't have anything to say. What we realized was that we had become conditioned to listen passively to what was broadcast over the airwaves, and only when "permitted" or "invited" to speak over an approved station were we able to prepare ourselves for such an event. Given that the airwaves were owned lock, stock, and barrel by commercial corporations, the likelihood that any of us would have thought through what we would say if the airwaves were ours was nonexistent.

It was only one year later that I took on the representation of Stephen Dunifer, aka Free Radio Berkeley, in what has already become a five-year battle with the Federal Communications Commission (FCC) over the question of who "owns" the airwaves. But let me digress to the way in which I got involved in the radio movement in the first place.

In 1991, I started working with a long-time friend, and political activist, Peter Franck. Peter and I had worked together in the National Lawyers Guild (NLG), a progressive bar association, for over twenty-five years. The preamble to the NLG's constitution identifies it as an organization founded upon the principle that "human rights shall be more sacred than property interests," not an altogether popular belief in this day of "free-market capitalism." Peter had formed a guild committee called the Committee on Democratic Communications (CDC). It was formed in response to a series of international gatherings, the MacBride Roundtables. These Roundtables focused on the problem facing the poor nations of the world that had to receive news and reporting about their local situations from New York, Tokyo, or London, instead of from their own national capitals.

The realization that entire nations had to depend upon receiving their news from the Western capitals was an appalling one. This north/south division (then described as Third World versus First World) arose as a result of the consolidation of media resources in a few international corporations that totally dominated the communications industry. Without access to the resources of these corporations, it was impossible for other nations to produce and create the sort of high-quality programming and news gathering that was found in the wealthy capitals of America, Europe, and Japan. The result was foreseeable. Western values and ideas dominated the medias of nations that had no equivalent outlets for their own broadcasts.

As the CDC investigated the implications of this phenomena for other areas of "democratic speech," it became obvious that all avenues of communication were the wholly owned property of private commercial interests. Newspapers, television stations, and radio licenses were the exclusive dominion of the rich. The rest of us expressed ourselves not by right, but by invitation. We discovered that the printing press had been licensed for years before people were free to print what they wanted, when they wanted to; that initial expenses for obtaining a radio license were as much as $100,000, in spite of the fact that the necessary equipment cost as little as $1,000; that newspaper ownership had dwindled to 1/100th of what it had been 100 years earlier. In short, we came to realize that the American people were voiceless. Rather than being participants in a dialogue, we had become passive recipients of what commercial corporations wanted to feed us. We understood that there was a significant difference between commercial speech and democratic dialogue. Whereas the former normally values efficiency, acceptability, and commonality, the latter frequently values dialogue, debate, and confrontation. To "sell" one is to abdicate the other.

At the same time that committee members were dividing up various responsibilities in our attempts to fight this monopolization, the FCC decided to go after Stephen Dunifer for his "pirate" radio broadcasts in Berkeley. It was our view that the real pirates were those who had stolen the airwaves from the American people and not the handful of microradio broadcasters who were attempting to take back a portion of the airwaves for local programming. As I became increasingly involved in communications law, I began to get a glimmer of the potential importance of radio as a means of two-way communication. As early as 1932, Bertolt Brecht had recognized the implications of what has now become an entire movement: "Radio could be the most wonderful public communication system imaginable . . . if it were capable, not only of transmitting, but of receiving, of making the listener not only hear but also speak."

Larry Soley first contacted me about the Dunifer case approximately two years ago. He was doing some investigative reporting on the case and had some questions about our strategy and goals. A year after our initial interview, I read the article that he wrote for *Covert Action Quarterly.* The article was not only an accurate description of what the case was about, but provided an overview that I had not seen in other articles. He was able to place the Free Radio Berkeley case in the broader political context that gave it meaning. When I saw the first draft of *Free Radio,* I was able to understand how he was able to accomplish that objective.

The current microradio movement did not arise in a vacuum. By setting forth the history of the movement, Soley enables the reader to understand why and how it has captured such momentum and power at this historical moment. As a tool for analyzing this history, Larry divides low-power stations into four categories: Clandestine (or guerrilla); pirate; micropower; and ghost. He then traces the development of each of these categories as they have progressed over the last half century. Just as Ben Bagdikian's book, *The Media Monopoly,* opened the door for a discussion of media ownership, and Robert McChesney's book, *Telecommunications, Mass Media and Democracy,* explained the history of why commercial radio today has become a form of intellectual pablum, Soley's book is, for the microradio movement, the antidote to the adage: "Those who ignore their history are bound to relive it."

Stephen Dunifer and Ron Sakolsky have also published a book titled, *Seizing the Airwaves, A Free Radio Handbook*. For those who would participate in the microradio movement of today, it is an essential document. It not only sets forth the schematics and technological information needed to start a microradio station but also contains articles and discussions from its current advocates and proponents.

All those who would pick up Stephen's and Ron's book should also understand the importance of reading *Free Radio*. Its descriptions of current struggles are both accurate and compelling. Regarding the history of Free Radio Berkeley, one has the impression that Soley was actually present while the strategy discussions were taking place and while the struggles were developing. When he is describing the anti-Nazi underground stations and other resistance stations, the book reads like an adventure novel. Most importantly, by understanding the rich variety of ways in which previous stations have provided vehicles for democratic communications, one can fully grasp the potential for a broadened microradio movement.

Louis N. Hiken

1

Freedom Calling

Of the major mass media—television, newspapers, magazines, and radio—radio is the most important and influential worldwide. Radio has over twice the penetration of television and nearly four times the penetration of newspapers. There is only one television set for every 6.7 persons in the world, but there is one radio receiver for every three people, making radio far more available. By contrast, newspapers have far lower penetration; there are about 522 million copies of newspapers produced daily, or about one newspaper per eleven people.[1]

Even in the United States, which has the largest number of television receivers and transmitters and the largest daily newspaper circulation, radio remains an exceedingly important medium. On average, U.S. adults listen to radio about 2.8 hours daily. Overall, there are about 5.6 radio receivers per household with about 96 percent of Americans listening to these radio receivers weekly.[2]

In the world there are nearly 27,500 radio transmitters sending out messages to listeners on the AM, FM, and shortwave bands. About 12,000 of these are in the United States. Despite the large number of radio transmitters, radio has been operated as a one-way medium of communication in nearly every country, with listeners consuming but not producing the programming to which they listen. Instead of allowing citizens and community groups to produce radio programming, most nations have placed broadcasting in the hands of government agencies, private corporations, or faceless bureaucracies, which decide what programs listeners will hear.

Types of Free Radio Stations

Because of the limits that most governments place on access to the airwaves, citizen activists in many nations have started their own radio stations, challenging the laws that have made radio a one-way communication medium. These unlicensed stations are known as *free radio* stations because they operate without gov-

1

ernment approval and are free of government-imposed limits on access to the radio spectrum.

Free radio stations are sometimes referred to as clandestine, pirate, micropower, or ghost stations, depending upon their purposes and operating frequencies. Clandestine stations, sometimes called *guerrilla* stations, advocate
revolution. They usually broadcast during periods of civil war or social rebellion, calling on citizens to overthrow their repressive overlords.[3] The stations
are usually operated by well-organized guerrilla groups in guerrilla-controlled
territory or by exiled political organizations.

Because clandestine stations broadcast their messages throughout a country,
they almost always broadcast from powerful transmitters, usually on the shortwave band. Examples of clandestine station currently on the air include the Radio
of the Sudan People's Liberation Army, operated by a guerrilla army battling
against the repressive Islamic government of the Sudan, and Radio Kudriat
Nigeria, operated by the National Liberation Council of Nigeria, an exiled group
opposed to Nigeria's military government.

Shortwave frequencies are used by clandestine stations because these radio
waves bounce off the ionized Kennelly-Heaviside layer and back to earth, allowing the signals to travel great distances. By using refracted rather than ground
wave transmission, clandestine stations can also conceal their transmitters' locations.

In contrast with clandestine stations, which advocate the overthrow of repressive governments, pirate stations are culturally oriented stations that carry music
and entertainment programs. They broadcast on AM, FM, and shortwave to entire cities, sometimes to even larger areas, and occasionally carry commercials,
which clandestine stations would never air. The raison d'etre of pirate stations is
that government-licensed stations often fail to carry enough music or entertainment programs of a certain type to satisfy listener needs. For example, numerous
pirate stations using names such as Witch City Radio and Voice of the Dead take
to the airwaves in the United States every Halloween, playing seasonal music such
as the Rolling Stones' "Sympathy for the Devil," tracks from films such as *Night of
the Living Dead,* and heavy metal music laced with satanic allusions. The stations
provide a holiday experience that is not available on most licensed stations. Other
pirate stations, such as the shortwave station WKND, appear on weekends, programming large doses of classic rock from groups such as Pink Floyd and the
Moody Blues. Still others, like WGAY in Milwaukee, play nonstop dance music.
The Milwaukee-based station often airs promotional announcements for *La
Cage,* a gay dance club. Many similar stations broadcast in Great Britain, playing
East Indian, Pakistani, and Caribbean music for foreign-born residents.[4]

The purpose of micropower or microradio stations is to change restrictive radio licensing laws while providing alternative news and information to specific
neighborhoods. Microradio stations usually broadcast on the FM band with limited power, making them audible within only a few miles of their transmitters,

which is how they got their name. Because they broadcast from low-cost, low-power transmitters that are easily assembled and operated, there are far more microradio stations in operation than there are clandestine stations.

Most micropower stations operate in open defiance of government licensing policies because the policies usually restrict the range of political viewpoints expressed over radio to those acceptable to government leaders. For example, a micropower station called Radio TeleVerdad has defied the Mexican government's control of the airwaves since 1995 by broadcasting pro-democracy commentaries in Mexico City. The station was raided by soldiers shortly after it signed on, but after protests by listeners and opposition politicians, it was allowed to resume broadcasting.[5] Just two years later, the opposition Democratic Revolutionary Party won Mexico City's elections for mayor and city assembly, assuring that Radio TeleVerdad will remain on the air for some time in the future.

Similar stations have operated in the United States, Argentina, the Philippines, and Belgium, sometimes with even greater success than in Mexico. In Belgium, the government was forced to change its licensing policies in 1981, legalizing the low-power FM stations that appeared in the late 1970s to protest the government's broadcasting monopoly. The Belgian government first responded to the free radio broadcasts with repression, but abandoned this policy when it became clear that its repression had failed. By 1980 nearly eighty free radio stations were on the air, openly defying the government. Many of these were operated by environmentalists, union militants, and peace activists.

Confronted by these protests and its own inability to silence the stations, the Belgian government decided to make them legal. By then, the broadcasters had formed an association—Association pour la Libération de Ondes-Belgique—and the number of low-power stations on the air soon multiplied. By 1987 there were nearly 300 of these stations broadcasting in the French-speaking regions of Belgium alone, giving voices to individuals and groups who had not previously had access to the airwaves.[6]

Lastly, *ghost* broadcasts are unlicensed transmissions that surreptitiously interrupt the broadcasts of licensed stations, providing an alternative view to that expressed by government-licensed stations. Ghosting was used by the Allies during World War II in an effort to break the German government's information monopoly. Radio addresses of Adolph Hitler were interrupted with laughter, boos, and hisses by Allied-operated ghost stations, and some ghost stations interrupted official German radio broadcasts with shouts of "Lies!" and "Don't believe it!"

More recently, a ghost broadcaster interrupted Long Island radio station WBAB's transmissions with music and calls to save the whales. The ghost transmission was picked up and relayed at Mitchell Field, where an estimated 150,000 people heard the broadcast while waiting for fireworks to begin on July 4, 1991. A year earlier, another ghost broadcaster appeared on the frequency used by Long Island station WALK. The broadcaster denounced the Federal Communications Commission (FCC), which regulates broadcasting in the United States.[7]

Radio, the "Reel" Alternative

Although free stations are often classified as either clandestine, pirate, micro-power, or ghost stations, these distinctions among the types of free stations are not truly discrete.[8] Many U.S. pirate stations, such as the Voice of Stench, which has operated sporadically on shortwave since 1989, feature political as well as musical programming. Since 1992 the Voice of Stench has featured talks by anar-chist-musicians such as the Dead Kennedys' Jello Biafra, in addition to punk rock music and lighter entertainment fare. Clandestine stations also carry musical pro-gramming in addition to political talks, and most microradio stations carry mu-sic and entertainment programming in addition to local news, community an-nouncements, and commentaries.

Regardless of how it is described, free radio broadcasting has emerged as a ma-jor tool for circumventing government restrictions on free expression. Radio, rather than newspapers, has became the most important free speech medium for several reasons. First, a radio transmitter can be constructed for far less than the cost of a printing press and composition equipment. Low-power transmitters can be constructed for just a few hundred dollars, making them accessible to Central American peasant revolutionaries and inner-city, hip-hop youth. Moreover, once the transmitter is obtained, only minimal expenses are needed to keep the station on the air. In contrast, newspapers require never-ending expenditures for ink, newsprint, and printing plates, making newspaper production a very costly en-deavor.

Second, newspapers and computers, unlike radio, require users to be literate. In Africa today, approximately three-fifths of the population is illiterate; in Asia, ap-proximately one-half is. Even in the United States, it is estimated that 20 percent of the population is functionally illiterate. Radio can easily be used by these peo-ple, whereas newspapers and computers cannot.

Third, for some demographic groups, like teens and young adults, radio is the medium of choice. It is personal, portable, and nonintrusive. Newspapers and television, on the other hand, are used more by older adults and children, who are unlikely targets of dissident political messages. To effectively reach many teens and young adults with protest messages, radio must be used.

Fourth, under conditions of political repression, it is safer to operate an illegal radio station than an underground newspaper. A transmitter can be moved easily from place to place, whereas composition equipment and printing presses are dif-ficult to move. In many places, such as present-day Burma, it is also difficult to obtain ink and paper, which are needed to produce a newspaper. Supplies such as these aren't necessary to produce an effective free radio broadcast.

Fifth, it is safer for citizens to listen to free radio stations than to read banned newspapers. Readers have to hide and eventually dispose of contraband newspa-pers, whereas radio broadcasts leave no artifact to betray their presence.

Sixth, radio receivers, compared to television sets and computers, are inexpensive. Although one copy of a newspaper might be inexpensive, newspapers must be purchased on an ongoing basis, which can add up to a considerable expense over time. But radios can be purchased for a few dollars, which means that even the poorest family can afford one. Consequently, radio has developed the highest penetration of any medium in the world. For example, in Mozambique, one of world's poorest countries, there is only one television set for every 418 persons and one daily newspaper available for every 1,000 persons, yet there is one radio for every 29 persons, making radio the most widely-disseminated medium.[9]

NOTES

1. Computed from data reported in *The World Fact Book 1996* (Washington, D.C.: Central Intelligence Agency, 1996) and *Statistical Yearbook, 41st Issue* (New York: United Nations, 1991).

2. S. Watson Dunn, Arnold M. Barban, Dean M. Krugman, and Leonard N. Reid, *Advertising,* 7th ed. (Chicago: The Dryden Press, 1990), p. 448.

3. Lawrence C. Soley and John S. Nichols, *Clandestine Radio Broadcasting* (New York: Praeger, 1986).

4. Andrew Yoder, *Pirate Radio* (Solana Beach, Calif.: High Text Publications, 1996), p. 194–195; Andrew Yoder, "The Radio Animal Still Hiking Up the Jolly Roger," *Popular Communications,* December 1991, p. 24; Lawrence Soley, "Milwaukee Pirates Challenge Narrow Music Formats," *Shepherd Express,* September 18, 1997, p. 11; Alex Spillius, "The Jungle Telegraph," *Guardian,* January 28, 1995, p. T12.

5. Kenneth Noble, "Rebel Radio Operator Exports His Know-how," *New York Times,* January 24, 1996, p. A10.

6. Phillip O. Keirstead and Sonia-Kay Keirstead, "The Many Faces of Community Radio," *International Communication Bulletin, 22* (1987): 8.

7. Heidi Durrow, "Hunt Is on for Pirate Radio Station," *Newsday,* July 5, 1991, p. 36.

8. For an example of how these stations are distinguished, see Sydney W. Head, *World Broadcasting Systems* (Belmont, Calif.: Wadsworth Publishing, 1985). Head defines clandestine stations as "secretive, unauthorized stations having political motives" and pirate stations as "unauthorized commercial stations, usually in international waters" (pp. 404, 414).

9. "Nations—Mozambique," *The World Almanac and Book of Facts 1994* (Mahwah, N.J.: Funk & Wagnalls, 1993), p. 791.

2

The Origins of Free Radio

Although the number of free stations on the air has surged in recent years—there are several thousand on the air today—free radio is not a new phenomenon. It is almost as old as radio broadcasting itself. The first free radio station surfaced in Czechoslovakia in February 1931, calling on workers to unite against the fascist leaders of Europe.[1] The station, which apparently operated from a mobile transmitter, broke the government's monopoly on broadcasting and called for a mass mobilization on February 26 in the Czech, German, and Hungarian languages.[2]

Czechoslovak authorities responded to the broadcasts by searching for the transmitter in the homes of well-known Communist party members, but never found it. The station simply disappeared, although a similar station surfaced in Budapest, Hungary two months later. The Hungarian station, like its Czech counterpart, carried speeches, commentaries, and coded messages directed at Communist party members. The Hungarian government also searched for the transmitter, but never located it. Like the earlier Czechoslovak station, this one disappeared as mysteriously as it appeared.[3]

On New Year's Eve, 1931, Germans listening to a radio address by aging president Paul von Hindenburg heard the speech interrupted by voices shouting slogans such as, "Let all proletarians unite in opposing the emergency decrees and the dictatorship." The voices were protesting restrictive laws that were to go into effect on New Year's Day.[4] While this was not the first time that dissidents had tampered with official German government radio broadcasts—they had previously cut off the transmissions—this is the first known example of ghost broadcasting, in which a free radio station operates on the same frequency as a government-approved broadcast, interrupting it.[5]

Free radio broadcasting quickly spread throughout the world during the 1930s as a method for reaching citizens with anti-government protest messages. In 1932 the Indian National Congress, which spearheaded the movement for Indian independence, started the Congress Broadcasting Station, which protested Great Britain's refusal to grant the country independence or dominion status.[6]

In 1933, encouraged by President Franklin D. Roosevelt's criticisms of Cuban leader Gerardo Machado, young Cubans organized demonstrations and protests against the Cuban dictator. In the midst of the protests a free radio station appeared, broadcasting anti-Machado commentaries and calling upon the Cuban army to join the rebellion. Although the government located the transmitter and arrested its operators, other freedom stations soon appeared. These stations also called upon the army to rebel, which it did, and Machado was ousted and forced into exile.

The same year in Barcelona, Spain, in the midst of a syndicalist-sponsored railway strike, a free radio station took to the airwaves, urging Catalan listeners to store up provisions in anticipation of an upcoming general strike.[7] And in Germany, following the Nazi party's rise to power, numerous free radio stations appeared. The German Socialists, banned from the airwaves, started a radio station inside Germany. After they were forced to flee, the Socialists established a transmitter that broadcast to the continent from a ship in the Baltic Sea.[8]

Another radio station, incorrectly identified by some writers as the world's first free radio station, was established by Nazi defector Otto Strasser.[9] Called Voice of the Black Front after Strasser's anti-Hitler Black Front organization, the station broadcast from a hotel in Zahori, Czechoslovakia, not far from the German border. It was operated by Rudolph Formis, who previously worked as an engineer for Stuttgart Radio. The station went off the air when Formis was murdered by Gestapo agents on January 24, 1935.[10]

The Saga of the *Freiheitssender*

Of the anti-Nazi stations broadcasting to Germany during the 1930s, none captured more attention than the *Deutscher Freiheitssender* (or "German Freedom Station"), which first appeared in January 1937, broadcasting uncensored programs to Nazi-controlled Germany on the 29.8-meter band. The station's first broadcast closed with the statement: "You will hear us tomorrow in spite of the secret police."[11]

True to its word, the station appeared at ten o'clock on subsequent nights. Several towns were searched to locate the transmitter, particularly in Baden, because the station intimated it was located there. But it was not found. German authorities soon learned that the station could be heard throughout Austria, Czechoslovakia, and Hungary, in addition to Germany, leading authorities to speculate that the station was located abroad. Nazi leaders first suggested that the freedom station broadcast from Minsk, near the Soviet-Polish border. In May, they reported that the transmitter was located in the west, in a woods in Luxembourg. Finally, Nazi leaders claimed the station was broadcasting from Moscow. In reality, but unknown to the German authorities, the station was based in Barcelona, Spain, where the Republican government was battling an insurgency led by Spanish general Francisco Franco, who received aid from Germany and Italy. The station was operated by German Communists who went to Spain to fight with the Republicans against Franco's troops. The station's operators included writers Gustav Regler and Alfred Kantorowicz.[12]

In an attempt to silence the Deutscher Freiheitssender, Germany started to jam it on March 23, placing a loud, disruptive signal on the 29.8-meter band. When the jamming started, the station announced: "We are moving. Follow us." It then moved to 30.8 meters. When jamming began on that frequency, the station moved again.

On April 10, 1937, representatives of the German Socialist, Communist, and Catholic parties met and formed an anti-Hitler coalition called the German People's Front. The People's Front was given responsibility for operating the Freedom Station. Thereafter, the Deutscher Freiheitssender opened its broadcasts with the announcement: "Hallo! Hallo! The anti-Fascist station is speaking."[13]

Novelist Heinrich Mann, brother of the more famous writer Thomas Mann, was chosen as chair of the German People's Front. Heinrich Mann was well-known in Germany, but barely known in the rest of Europe, despite having written several highly acclaimed novels. After becoming chair of the People's Front, Mann wrote a number of appeals that were broadcast by the Freedom Station. Mann's appeals persuaded others to write for it, including novelist Lion Feuchtwanger, painter Eugen Spiro, and poets Rudolf Leonhard and Bertolt Brecht. Brecht wrote the *German Satires*, a group of free-verse poems, specifically for broadcasting over the station.[14]

The contributions of celebrities like Lion Feuchtwanger and Bertolt Brecht attracted substantial attention to the Deutscher Freiheitssender, both within and outside Germany. In Germany, the government heightened its efforts to jam the station because it quickly became a symbol of anti-Nazi opposition. Other opponents of Hitler, believing it possible to successfully operate underground radio stations inside Germany, put their own stations on the air. These stations, like the station that inspired them, were also referred to as German Freedom Stations.

Many of the anti-Nazis who operated these stations were arrested. For example, in January 1939 Ernst Niekisch and several of his followers were arrested and imprisoned for operating a mobile radio station. Niekisch, like Otto Strasser, was a conservative opponent of Hitler. He was sentenced to life imprisonment at hard labor by Nazi courts, but was freed by the Allies in 1945. By that time, he was blind and paralyzed as a result of being used as a guinea pig for Nazi experiments.[15]

Soon after Germany occupied Austria, several freedom stations broadcasting from mobile transmitters appeared there. The first station called for Austrian troops to mutiny in the event of war and kept Austrians and the world informed about Nazi repression. "Austrians don't fight in a foreign uniform or in a foreign cause," the station declared. Many Austrian troops apparently heeded this call; troops mutinied in Graz, Innsbruck, and Vienna, and thousands deserted.

According to writer Charles Rolo, the Gestapo, assisted by technicians from German radio, eventually tracked down the station, finding it hidden beneath boxes of eggs and butter in a delivery truck. As the Gestapo moved in, the station's operators fled; one was shot and killed and the other two escaped to the Czechoslovakia, where they started another, short-lived freedom station. After Czechoslovakia was occupied, this station was silenced, but another soon appeared.[16] This one, too, was eventually forced off the air.

Despite the arrest of Niekisch and the Austrian broadcasters, the Deutscher Freiheitssender continued to broadcast. What silenced the station was not the arrest of individuals, but the defeat of the Spanish Republic by Franco's army. On January 26, 1939, Barcelona fell to Franco. On March 28, Madrid fell. The Spanish government, along with many anti-Nazi Germans, fled the country, thus silencing the station.[17]

But the Deutscher Freiheitssender was not silent for long. On August 31, 1939, the infamous Hitler-Stalin Pact was signed and on September 1, Germany attacked Poland. In response, England and France declared war on Germany. However, no fighting erupted between Germany and its opponents until the following year. During this period of "phony war," the French government allowed Willi Munzenberg, a Marxist publisher who opposed the Hitler-Stalin Pact, to resurrect the German Freedom Station from a location just outside Paris.[18]

Munzenberg's Freedom Station, like the original Deutscher Freiheitssender, operated on 29.8 meters. The station called on Germans to overthrow Hitler with speeches such as: "German people, for years we have suffered unbearable hardships, only to be dragged into Hitler's war. . . . Through the deeds of Hitler, the German nation is hated all over the world, but Germany will know how to deal with the Nazis. It is our duty to finish [off] these beasts in human form. . . . Germans, put an end to these swine."[19]

This version of the Freedom Station, unlike the original, was anti-Communist in addition to being anti-Nazi. Although the station was anti-Communist, it was nevertheless pro-socialist, and even broadcast communiqués of the American Socialist party.[20]

The Freiheitssender Melodramas

Inspired by patriotic duty—and by a desire to profit from the war and the Freiheitssender's fame—Two Cities Film Company in England produced a 1941 film about the Freedom Station called *The Voice in the Night*. The content of the film was completely fictitious, despite its advertisements, which promised "the fantastic truth behind today's sensational headlines."[21]

The hero of *The Voice in the Night* is an Austrian physician whose patients include the Führer. The doctor is sickened after witnessing the murder of a clergyman by his brother-in-law, a brutal storm trooper. The hero's revulsion turns to anti-Nazi activism after he learns that the fiancée of a young radio technician named Hans Glaser was raped by a Gestapo officer. Nazi authorities sent the rape victim to a concentration camp rather than punishing the criminal.

The physician and Hans Glaser, having had enough of Nazi bestiality, start an illegal radio station—the Freedom Station. In the film, the underground broadcasters manage to stay one step in front of the Gestapo, which ceaselessly tracks the mobile transmitter with direction-finding equipment. Near the end of the film, the doctor's anti-Nazi activities are revealed to the Gestapo and he is arrested and executed. Just when Nazi officials announce that the Freedom Station has been silenced, Hans Glaser comes out of hiding. He turns the hidden transmitter on and announces: "This is the Freedom Radio. . . . We shall be on the air tomorrow as usual."

Hollywood also produced a completely fictitious film about the German Freedom Station. This film, titled *Underground*, opened to better reviews than *The Voice in the Night*. The film is about Eric Franken, an anti-Nazi activist, whose brother Kurt is a loyal Nazi. Kurt falls in love with a woman in the German underground, which operates the Freedom Station. Upon learning of her involvement with the Freedom Station, Kurt turns the woman and her colleagues in to the Gestapo. After she and Eric Franken are executed, Kurt changes sides, taking his brother's place on the staff of the German Freedom Station.[22]

By the time *The Voice in the Night* and *Underground* were released, the real German Freedom Station was silent. In May 1940 Germany attacked France, ending the phony war. French resistance quickly collapsed, and the anti-Nazi government of Paul Reynaud was replaced by the pro-German government of Henri Philippe Pétain. Pétain's government silenced the Deutscher Freiheitssender and arrested Willi Munzenberg. Munzenberg escaped, but while making his way to freedom was murdered by Soviet NKVD or German Gestapo agents.[23]

Rather than ending the free radio movement, the shooting war in Europe led to the creation of even more free radio stations, most of which were operated by exiled or underground groups. One such station, called *Sender der Europaischen Revolution,* was operated by a group of German neo-Marxists called *Neubeginnen* (New Beginning), formed by dissident Communists and left-wing Socialists who went underground before Hitler eliminated his lawful opponents.[24] The group attempted to organize anti-Hitler opposition within the labor movement after the Nazi putsch and were moderately successful, but the Gestapo eventually arrested and executed most of its members. *Neubeginnen* members went into exile, first in France and then, after Germany's occupation of France, in Great Britain.

There Richard Crossman, an influential socialist, put a transmitter at the disposal of *Neubeginnen* members, who broadcast anti-Hitler programs to Germany between 1940 and 1942. The station implored German workers to sabotage war production, slow down assembly lines, and strike. Although the station was on British soil, the group produced and broadcast its own programs free of British dictates.[25]

Across the Irish Sea, the Irish Republican Army (IRA) operated a free radio station from a transmitter obtained in Germany. The station urged Catholics to remain neutral in the war. The station's transmitter was eventually located with the assistance of Military Intelligence, and its operators were arrested.[26] On the continent, anti-Nazi groups, such as Marshal Tito's Yugoslav partisans, operated free stations with names such as Radio Free Yugoslavia.[27]

Ersatz Freedom Stations

World War II also gave rise to a host of ersatz freedom stations—stations that claimed to be free radio stations, but were actually Axis- or Allied-sponsored operations. The ersatz freedom stations were put on the air because the pre-war free stations that they copied had been effective in circumventing censorship and mobilizing their audiences. The Allied and Axis powers, not recognizing that free radio stations were the outgrowth of legitimate opposition movements, believed that their ersatz radio stations would be similarly effective. In reality they could not be, since they were not the voices of real political movements. For example, Nazi Germany operated a station called *Voix de la Paix,* which claimed to be the underground radio station of a French pacifist movement. The station's real purpose was to sow defeatism and fear, not to mobilize a peace movement. There is little evidence that many people believed or even listened to the station.

Germany operated a similar station called Worker's Challenge, which broadcast to Great Britain. It claimed to broadcast from a hidden transmitter in England, but was actually broadcasting from the Rhineland and, later, Holland. The station's announcers said that they were socialist factory workers who opposed the war, but in reality they were expatriate British Nazis, whose caricatures of socialists were transparent to everybody but themselves. The station garnered little listenership, except for a few elderly gents who chuckled at the speakers' vulgarity, which, according to the *Times* of London, appeared "with unfailing regularity in front of every noun."[28]

Great Britain also operated ersatz freedom stations. *Gustav Siegfried Eins* claimed to be a station operated by a loyal Nazi sergeant, who sprinkled his diatribes with curses and allusions to Nazi corruption. Other British-operated ersatz freedom stations broadcast to Norway, Denmark, Belgium, Italy, and France.[29]

Germany's ally, Japan, sponsored ersatz freedom broadcasts to India, using the names Free India Radio, Radio Himalaya, and Radio Hindustani. The broadcasts encouraged anti-British activities in India. Japan was also the recipient of ersatz freedom station broadcasts. The U.S. Office of Strategic Services, the predecessor of the Central Intelligence Agency (CIA), operated a station called Voice of the People, which claimed to broadcast from inside Japan on shortwave. Voice of the People said that it was operated by loyal Japanese who believed that the best way to save Japan from defeat was to negotiate peace with the Allies. Broadcasts of this station were actually produced in the United States by Americans of Japanese descent, who were freed from internment camps to work on the station. Their recordings were flown from the United States to Saipan, where they were transmitted to Japan.[30]

Ersatz freedom stations continue to operate. For example, the CIA sponsored several ersatz freedom stations that broadcast to Panama prior to the U.S. invasion of that country in 1989. The stations were named *Radio Constitucional,* Voice of Freedom, and Voice of Liberty, and they carried programs critical of Panamanian strongman, General Manuel Noriega.[31] The stations claimed that they defended democracy, but they were really designed to prepare Panamanians for a U.S. invasion.

For operating Voice of Liberty, Panamanian authorities arrested a U.S. citizen, Kurt Frederick Muse, whose wife worked for the U.S. Defense Department. *Washington Post* reporter Bob Woodward, in his book, *The Commanders,* describes Muse as a CIA operative. Panama said that Muse confessed to operating the station and storing about $350,000 worth of radio transmitting equipment in several Panama City apartments. Although the CIA denied any connection with Muse, which is standard agency procedure, his jail was one of the first buildings seized by U.S. troops when they invaded Panama, and Muse was quickly freed and whisked back to Washington.

The Soviet Union also sponsored ersatz freedom stations. For example, the Soviet Union operated an ersatz freedom station called Radio Vltava, named for a river in Prague. The station broadcast during the Soviet invasion of Czechoslovakia in 1968 that ousted reform Communist leader Alexander Dubcek. The station, whose announcers spoke Slovak and Czech with Russian accents, claimed to be broadcasting from within Czechoslovakia. Radio Vltava thanked the Soviet Union for invading, claiming the action saved the country from "counter-revolution."[32]

NOTES

1. Czechoslovakia was ruled by a liberal democratic government during this period, rather than a fascist regime. Not until Emil Hácha became president in 1938 did Czechoslovakia have a true fascist government. Nevertheless, the government of Tomás Masaryk (1918–1935), like other European governments, maintained a centralized national broadcasting system.

2. "Red's Secret Radio Station Is Hunted in Czechoslovakia," *New York Times,* March 19, 1931, p. 11.

3. "Reds' Radio Mystifies," *New York Times,* April 26, 1931, p. 3E.

4. "Hindenburg on Radio Warns of Burdening Reich too Heavily," *New York Times,* January 1, 1932, p. 1.

5. Authorities in Germany concluded that the protestors had interrupted the broadcast by tapping into a telephone line rather than broadcasting on the same frequency as the von Hindenburg transmission. According to the report, the protestors entered a manhole outside Berlin, where they tapped into the telephone cable. If true, the interruption was not a

true "ghost" transmission. See "Hindenburg Urges World to Cut Arms," *New York Times*, January 2, 1932, p. 4. Nevertheless, true ghosting did first appear in 1932. That year, the German Communist party sponsored an illegal station that "disturbed the harmony of official broadcasts." See "Communist Activities in Berlin," *Times* (London), November 30, 1932, p. 11d.

6. "Congress Secret Wireless," *Times* (London), October 4, 1932, p. 13b.

7. "Goal Riot at Cordoba," *Times* (London), January 16, 1933, p. 12b.

8. Research Project on Totalitarian Communication, *German Freedom Stations Broadcasting to Britain* (New York: Research Project on Totalitarian Propaganda, 1942), pp. 7–8. The Communist party also operated an underground, anti-Hitler station, according to "Illegal Radio Station of Reds Seized by the Berlin Police," *New York Times*, December 9, 1932, p. 28.

9. In *The Black Game* (London: Michael Joseph, 1982), Ellic Howe wrote that the "first identifiable short-wave clandestine station was the one operated for Otto Strasser in Czechoslovakia in 1934–5" (p. 58).

10. Otto Strasser, *Flight from Terror* (New York: Robert M. McBride & Company, 1943); Douglas Reed, *The Prisoner of Ottawa* (London: Jonathan Cape, 1953), pp. 150–157.

11. F. Elwyn Jones, *The Defense of Democracy* (New York: E. P. Dutton & Co., 1938), pp. 250–255; "Red Radio Station Heard in Germany," *New York Times*, March 21, 1937, p. 11; Heinrich Fraenkel, *The German People Versus Hitler* (London: George Allen & Unwin, 1940), pp. 239–252.

12. Allan Merson, *Communist Resistance in Nazi Germany* (London: Lawrence and Wishart, 1985), p. 121; "Letter from R. A. Butler to the Viscount Halifax" (December 23, 1939) and replies, Foreign Office Series 317/24306, Public Records Office (Richmond, Surrey); Hans Teubner, "Der Deutsche Freiheitssender 29,8 — ein Fuhrungsorgan der KPD im Antifaschisteischen Kampf," *Militarwesen* 9 (1965):176–188.

13. Representative in Great Britain of the German Freedom Station, *Freedom Calling* (London: Frederick Muller, Ltd., 1939), p. 15.

14. Ibid., pp. 20–21; Martin Esslin, *Brecht: A Choice of Evils* (London: Eyre & Spottiswoode, 1982), pp. 59, 102.

15. "Nazis Locate Mystery Radio, Try 21 for Urging Hitler's Fall," *Washington Post*, January 4, 1939, pp. 1, 2; "Berlin Treason Trial Involves 'Pirate' Radio," *New York Herald Tribune*, January 4, 1939, p. 2; "Niekisch Gets Life Term for Anti-Nazi Plot," *New York Herald Tribune*, January 11, 1939, p. 10; Fabian von Schlabrendorff, *The Secret War Against Hitler* (New York: Pitman Publishing, 1965), p. 54.

16. Charles J. Rolo, *Radio Goes to War* (New York: G. P. Putnam's Sons, 1942), p. 222–223; "New Secret Austrian Radio Station," *CBS Monitoring Reports*, Report of October 29, 1939 (Microfilm Room, Library of Congress, Washington, D.C.), p. 6, No. 1613.

17. Helmut Pfanner reports that Kantorowicz had left Spain for France in 1938. Helmut Pfanner, *Exile in New York* (Detroit: Wayne State University Press, 1983), p. 214.

18. Sefton Delmer, *Black Boomerang* (London: Secker & Warburg, 1962), p. 40.

19. "German Freedom Station," *British Broadcasting Corporation Monitoring Reports*, Report of November 19, 1939, p. 1D.

20. "German Freedom Station on 29.8," *CBS Monitoring Report*, November 11, 1939, p. 7.

21. The description is based on the following film reviews: Donald Kirkely, "Freedom Radio," *Baltimore Sun,* June 30, 1941, p. 16; "At the Globe," *New York Times,* May 23, 1941, p. 25; and "The Voice in the Night," *New York Post,* May 23, 1941, p. 12. The film reviewer for the *Daily Worker* denounced the film as "a choice bit of hypocrisy" that covers up "the British big shots' responsibility for Naziism." See Milton Meltzer, "'The Voice in the Night' Mangles Current History," *Daily Worker,* May 24, 1941, p. 8. Less than a month after this review appeared, Germany invaded the Soviet Union, leading the Communist party to rally to the defense of the Soviets' new ally, England.

22. Leo Miskin, "Globe Brings Another Anti-Nazi Thriller in Warners' 'Underground,'" *Morning Telegraph,* June 23, 1941, p. 9; "Underground," *Baltimore Sun,* August 4, 1941, p. 6; "'Underground,' A Film Dealing with Radio Anti-Nazi Activities Seen at Globe," *New York Times,* June 23, 1941, p. 13.

23. Delmer, *Black Boomerang,* p. 40; Ruth Fischer, *Stalin and German Communism* (Cambridge: Harvard University Press, 1948).

24. For a discussion of the *Neubeginnen,* see Lewis J. Edinger, *German Exile Politics* (Los Angeles: University of California Press, 1956), pp. 82–88, 164–168.

25. Delmer, *Black Boomerang.*

26. Carolle J. Carter, *The Shamrock and the Swastika* (Palo Alto, Calif.: Pacific Books, 1977), p. 104.

27. Vladimir Dedijer, *The Battle Stalin Lost* (New York: Grosset and Dunlap, 1971), pp. 52–54.

28. "'Billingsgate' on the Air," *Times* (London) August 21, 1940, p. 4; J. A. Cole, *Lord Haw-Haw & William Joyce* (New York: Farrar, Straus & Giroux, 1964), pp. 161–163; Research Project on Totalitarian Communication, *German Freedom Stations Broadcasting to Britain* (New York: Research Project on Totalitarian Communication, 1942).

29. The British-sponsored stations are discussed in Ellic Howe, *The Black Game* (London: Michael Joseph, 1982) and W. J. West, *The Truth Betrayed* (London: Duckworth, 1987).

30. Lawrence Soley, *Radio Warfare* (New York: Praeger, 1989); Lawrence Soley and Sheila O'Brien, "Clandestine Broadcasting in the Southeast Asian Peninsula," *International Communication Bulletin,* 22(1987): 13–20.

31. Lawrence Soley, "Clandestine Radio and the End of the Cold War," *Media Studies Journal* 7 (1993): 129–138.

32. Robert Littell, ed., *The Czech Black Book* (New York: Praeger, 1969).

3

Free Radio and
National Liberation

Radio played an even more important role after World War II. Radio receivers had become more widely available internationally, radio had become the principle information source to much of the world's population during the war, and radio transmitters had become more accessible to dissident groups. In 1934, for example, there were 42 million radio receivers in the world. Only 100,000 of these were in Africa, 2 million in Asia, and 900,000 in Latin America. By 1949 there were 160 million receivers worldwide with 2 million in Africa, 8 million in Asia, and 6.5 million in Latin America.[1] Radio penetration had grown quickly during World War II because it was an efficient, safe, and inexpensive method for obtaining information, which could be easily assessed for accuracy by comparing the information provided by one station, such as the Overseas Service of the British Broadcasting Corporation (BBC), with that of another, such as Radio Moscow.

Radio transmitters were also more widely available after the end of World War II, making them more accessible to opposition and underground groups such as the Greek National People's Liberation Army (ELAS), a large, left-leaning guerrilla group that fought a hit-and-run war against the German occupation of Greece during World War II. The ELAS started a free radio station soon after Great Britain attempted to establish its control over Greece, following Germany's withdrawal from the country. British attempts to impose a conservative government on Greece precipitated a civil war, which marked the beginning of the modern period of free radio broadcasting. The ELAS station, Free Greece Radio, demonstrated the importance of free radio in situations of conflict and civil war. Indeed, the United States responded to the conflict with the Truman Doctrine, a policy that justified military intervention in countries where the United States perceived its interests to be threatened. The Truman Doctrine was the rationale for later U.S. military intervention in Lebanon, Vietnam, El Salvador, and elsewhere.

Free Radio and Civil War

In May 1944 as German troops prepared to withdraw from Greece, Great Britain sponsored a conference of Greek political parties in Lebanon, where a post-war government headed by exiled leader Georgios Papandreou was created. The coalition government promised freedom of speech and assembly for Greek political parties and placed guerrilla armies such as the ELAS at the disposal of the government.

On October 18, 1944, following Germany's withdrawal, Papandreou returned to Greece, escorted by British troops under the command of General Ronald Scobie, who began negotiating with the ELAS on how it could be integrated into a national army. Less than two months later, General Scobie, believing that the guerrillas threatened British interests in Greece, ordered the ELAS to immediately demobilize. In response, ELAS supporters in the coalition government resigned and called for protest demonstrations and a general strike. The Greek government responded to the demonstrations by sending in police, who opened fire on the protesters, triggering an even wider confrontation.

In the midst of the conflict, Radio Free Greece appeared, announcing, "This is Athens calling . . . the voice of the Greek National Liberation Front." The station's first broadcast was directed to the "liberal peoples of the world," whom the station implored to support the ELAS. Another broadcast was addressed to the "English Labor Party, asking it to denounce British actions in Greece," reporting that Britain was attempting "to install a fascist dictatorship, using officially and openly the very methods of the Germans." The broadcast was true; the strongest supporters of the British action in Greece were collaborators who had worked with the Nazis during the period of German occupation.

The ELAS, poorly equipped and trained as a hit-and-run guerrilla army rather than a conventional fighting force, was little match for the well-equipped British army, which drove the ELAS from Athens and surrounding regions. Outgunned, the ELAS signed the Varkiza Agreement with the Greek government and its British protectors on February 12, 1945. The agreement stipulated that the ELAS would disband, that free and open elections would be scheduled, and that the Greek Communist and other leftist parties would be free to operate openly in Greece.

The ELAS did disband and it turned over much of its weaponry (but not its transmitter) to the Greek government. That was about the only aspect of the Varkiza Agreement that was fulfilled. Rather than allowing leftist parties to openly operate, Greek police and national guardsmen, cooperating with former Nazi collaborators, launched a "white terror" against former ELAS members. Leftist rallies were disrupted, newsprint to left-wing newspapers was restricted, printing presses of leftist newspapers were smashed, and numerous people were assassinated.[2] The right-wing actions demonstrated the vulnerability of the newspapers that were used for organizing resistance; the equipment was difficult to move, easily located and demolished by thugs, and once destroyed, nearly impossible to replace. Moreover, the supply of paper needed to print a newspaper was easily cut off, making printing presses useless.

As a result of the terror, leftist parties boycotted the scheduled parliamentary elections, and former ELAS guerrillas were forced to abandon their towns for the safety of the mountains. In this atmosphere of intimidation, the right-wing won the parliamentary elections and quickly passed a series of restrictive laws. Special courts were established to try people charged with "subversive activities" and leftist newspapers were banned. Despite these actions, the Greek government continued to receive assistance from Great Britain and the United States, the latter eventually becoming the Greek government's chief sponsor.

The ELAS members who escaped to the countryside slowly coalesced into a guerrilla army called the Democratic Army of Greece. On July 16, 1947, the Democratic Army resurrected its old radio station, this time called the Radio Station of the Democratic Army of Greece. The first broadcast announced that "from today, the Democratic Army of Greece and with it the Greek people have their own powerful radio station . . . 'The Voice of Truth' will be heard . . . twice daily at 12:01 a.m. and 1:00 p.m." The station remained on the air throughout the Greek civil war.

It was through the broadcasts of the Radio Station of the Democratic Army of Greece that the reinvigorated ELAS stayed in touch with the outside world and informed sympathetic Greeks in cities about events in the countryside. For example, the station informed the world about the Greek government's massacre of "more than thirty women, children, and prisoners" near Nigrita, where government troops "burned about twenty-five houses." Over the station's airwaves, the Democratic Army announced that it was establishing its own government, which "granted men and women complete equality; prohibited discrimination against people for their race, religion, nationality, or opinions; and full national rights to minorities."

As the civil war escalated, President Harry Truman declared Greece to be pivotal in the worldwide fight against Communism and, in a speech asking Congress to provide the Greek government with massive funding, declared that the Democratic Army was a terrorist group "of several thousand men, led by Communists." The speech enunciated the Truman Doctrine, which consisted of propping up right-wing regimes and using military force to stop leftist and insurgency forces.

As the Greek military machine expanded in size and strength with the influx of U.S. aid, the Democratic Army secretly moved many bases and even its radio transmitter from Greece to neighboring Yugoslavia to keep them from being bombed by Greek government planes. Locating the transmitter outside Greece turned out to be a costly mistake. At the same that the Greek army was getting a massive armaments infusion from the United States, the feud between Stalin and Tito was escalating. The feud was caused by Soviet leader Josef Stalin's attempts to impose his totalitarian version of socialism on Yugoslavia and other East European nations.

The Greek Communist party, which was a major but not the only force in the Democratic Army, backed Stalin rather than President Josip Broz Tito of Yugoslavia. Fearing that the Democratic Army could become the nucleus of an anti-Tito army within Yugoslavia, Tito ordered the Greek guerrillas to close their bases and leave.

Tito's decision not only forced the Democratic Army to move its transmitter from Yugoslavia, but it cut the army's supply lines and diminished its military capacity. Other errors, such as attempting to turn the Democratic Army from a guerrilla force into a conventional military army, diluted the Democratic Army's strength and eventually led to its defeat.

One of the most costly lessons of the Greek civil war is that free radio operators cannot depend on the largesse of a friendly government for support. This is a lesson that several other groups have also learned—usually the hard way. During the early 1970s, the Palestine Liberation Organization (PLO) depended upon the Egyptian, Syrian, and other Arab governments for the use of radio transmitters, from which it broadcast the Voice of Palestine. Its Egyptian-based transmitters were shut down in 1973 after a Damascus-based PLO station broadcast criticism of Egypt's increasingly friendly relations with the United States. The PLO had similar experiences with other Arab governments. As a result of these incidents, the PLO acquired its own transmitter, from which it eventually made broadcasts free from Arab government censorship.[3]

Other Post–World War II Free Stations

Although the Democratic Army and its radio station were silenced, this was not the fate of other free radio stations that operated during the immediate post–World War II era. In Costa Rica and Indonesia, the operators of free radio stations emerged victorious, and their illegal free stations either emerged from the underground to became legal, *aboveground* stations, or were silenced when the victorious rebels took control of official broadcasting stations.

During the 1940s, Costa Rica was ruled by an authoritarian, right-wing politician, Dr. Rafael Angel Calderon, who maintained control through an alliance with the opportunistic Costa Rican Communist party. The Communists justified the alliance by claiming that it was in keeping with their Popular Front strategy, which sought to ally all anti-fascists. Although the alliance effectively kept Axis supporters out of government, it also disenfranchised many Costa Ricans.

A disenfranchised farmer and socialist, "Don Pepe" Jose Figueres Ferrer, alarmed by the president's authoritarian policies, purchased time on a Costa Rican commercial radio station and denounced the president. Even before his speech was finished, Costa Rican police raided the station, arrested Don Pepe, and exiled him to Mexico. In Mexico, Don Pepe came into contact with other exiled

Central Americans, who formed a loosely-knit group called the Caribbean Legion. The legion became dedicated to ousting Caribbean dictators Rafael Trujillo of the Dominican Republic, the Somoza family of Nicaragua, and Calderon in Costa Rica.[4]

After Calderon declared himself victor after being beaten in the 1948 presidential election, Don Pepe and other armed legionnaires launched an insurrection against Calderon from a base camp in southern Costa Rica. Guatemala aided the insurgents, providing them with logistical support, arms, and a radio transmitter, from which the revolutionaries broadcast The Voice of Liberty from their base camp. The free station's signature tune was the familiar opening notes of Beethoven's Fifth Symphony, which the BBC had used during World War II to begin its broadcasts. In Morse code, the beginning notes signify "V" for "Victory."

The Voice of Liberty was on the air for forty-five days—the length of the Costa Rican civil war. The station provided listeners with political commentary and tactical advice. The station explained the ideology of the revolutionaries and promised that the "day that we end the war against bad faith, we shall begin a new war: the war against poverty."[5] The station also gave instructions on how listeners could participate in the insurrection, something subsequent free stations have also done. The Voice of Liberty instructed listeners to build barricades on roads and cut communication lines, thus hampering the movement of government troops.[6]

In the end the insurrectionists won, despite intervention by Nicaraguan dictator Anastasio Somoza, who sent 500 troops across the border to aid Calderon. Calderon was forced into exile and Figueres established a democratic government, much to the chagrin of regional dictators like Somoza. Indeed, Somoza was so alarmed by the presence of a democratic government in Costa Rica that he schemed to replace Figueres's government with an autocratic regime and even sponsored an ersatz freedom station called the Voice of the Authentic Anti-Communist Revolutionary Army, to call for Figueres's ouster. Like the calls from most ersatz freedom stations, these went unheeded.

Under Don Pepe and other democratically elected leaders, Costa Rica prospered, achieving Central America's highest standard of living, in part by abolishing its army and forcing the United Fruit Company, the large, U.S.-owned banana-growing corporation, to improve pay and working conditions for Costa Rican employees. While Costa Rica prospered, Nicaragua stagnated socially and economically. In the end, Anastasio Somoza was assassinated; later, his family was ousted from power by Sandinista guerrillas, who operated a free radio station called the Voice of Sandino during that country's civil war.

Free Radio and National Independence

In contrast with the Voice of Liberation and the Voice of Sandino, which operated during internal civil wars, the Voice of Free Indonesia operated as part of an anti-colonial struggle, where indigenous peoples sought to expel a European colonial power—in this case, the Netherlands.

Prior to World War II, Indonesia, a country consisting of over thirteen thousand islands, was a colony of the Netherlands called the Dutch Indies. It was administered by Dutch authorities and western-educated Indonesians and Chinese, whose migration to Indonesia was encouraged by the Dutch to dilute nationalist sympathies. In 1942, in the midst of World War II, Indonesia was occupied by Japan, which interned the Dutch administrators. In the hopes of securing Indonesian assistance in fighting the Allies, Japan replaced the Dutch administrators with indigenous peoples, granted Indonesia limited self-government, promised independence after the war, and provided local militias with arms and training. As a result, Indonesian nationalists were in a position to declare their country independent after Japan's defeat.

On the morning of August 17, 1945, three days after Japan's unconditional surrender, Indonesia declared itself independent, with Indonesian Nationalist party leaders Sukarno and Muhammad Hatta as president and vice-president. Few Indonesians were aware of the declaration or of Japan's surrender, since neither were announced on the local Japanese-controlled radio stations.[7] The declaration of independence was not recognized by Great Britain, whose troops were scheduled to land in Indonesia in September to accept the Japanese surrender there. Neither was it recognized by France—which hoped to reassert colonial control in Indochina, also occupied by Japan during the war—or by the Netherlands, which expected to again become Indonesia's colonial master.

Because Indonesia is formed from many islands where literacy is low and newspapers scarce, most Indonesians did not hear about their country's declaration of independence until September. When they did hear, it was by word-of-mouth or from the broadcasts of the Voice of Free Indonesia, a rebel broadcasting station started by members of the Youth Generation of Indonesia, an organization of pro-independence students. The free station was started in early September to inform Indonesia's dispersed population about independence and to mobilize support for the declaration. The station urged Indonesians to seize arms, buildings, and communication and transportation systems from the Japanese. Soon, supporters of independence were in control of "the railway and tram systems, the telephone exchange, and an increasing number of private and public institutions."[8]

The free station changed its frequency constantly to avoid being located by Japanese authorities, who were required under the terms of the surrender to maintain order in Japanese-occupied areas. The rebel radio station denounced Japan and the West for failing to support Indonesian independence and announced that the rebels would fight for independence. Indonesian rebels detained and disarmed Japanese troops in many areas and fought British troops after they landed in Bandung, Surabaya, and other areas of the country.[9] Throughout, the Voice of Free Indonesia kept Indonesians and the world informed about events.

Great Britain, which was using detachments of Indian troops to occupy Indonesia while simultaneously confronting an independence movement in India, informed the Dutch government that it would not fight a war in Indonesia to protect Dutch interests, given its problems in India. Under pressure from Great Britain, the Netherlands signed the Linggajati Agreement, which recognized Sukarno as head of the government on three islands, with the Dutch queen the symbolic head of a greater federation of Indonesia. The agreement gave the new government its own radio stations, so the free radio signed off. However, the Dutch soon abrogated the Linggajati Agreement, invaded and occupied several islands, and blockaded others. The new government was able to circumvent the blockade and communicate with the outside world using its newly acquired broadcasting stations. This helped bring international pressure on the Netherlands, which eventually, but reluctantly, relinquished its claims to Indonesia.

Free Radio Worldwide

Free radio slowly spread throughout the world during the years immediately following World War II. In Vietnam, shortly after free radio appeared in Indonesia, Vietminh rebels started an anti-French free station called Voice of the South. To avoid being captured by French troops, the station's operators moved their bulky transmitter daily. This station operated between 1947, shortly after the anti-colonial war with the French began, and 1954, when the Geneva Accords were signed and the conflict temporarily halted. In Burma, a free radio station called Radio Kawthulay, named for the Karen ethnic minority region, appeared in 1949. The station demanded greater autonomy for the Karen region, to which the government agreed after two years of civil conflict. Radio Kawthulay operated throughout the conflict.[10]

It was during the late 1950s and early 1960s that free radio broadcasting grew rapidly. During the Soviet invasion of Hungary, backers of Communist premier Imre Nagy operated free radio stations that denounced the Soviet intervention. One station, Radio Rajk, named for a Hungarian Communist leader who was framed and executed by Stalin's henchmen in 1949, announced, "We Hungarian Communists will find out who, and under what circumstances, asked for the intervention of Soviet troops, and the guilty will get the place they deserve—the gallows." The station never had the opportunity to carry out its pledge; the Soviets hunted down the station operators and other opponents of the Soviet intervention and executed many, including Imre Nagy.

In Algeria, beginning in 1957 the National Liberation Front (FLN) operated a free radio station that opposed French colonial rule. Until the Voice of Struggling Algeria took to the airwaves, Algerians rarely acquired or listened to radio receivers because radio consisted of "Frenchmen speaking to Frenchmen," according to author Frantz Fanon, author of *The Wretched of the Earth* and *Studies in a*

Dying Colonialism.[11] After the FLN's station went on the air, Algerians quickly acquired radio receivers. Within twenty days of the appearance of the Voice of Struggling Algeria, the entire stock of radio receivers in Algeria was sold out. The French, realizing the power of free radio, soon banned the sale of radio receivers and batteries and started jamming the FLN broadcasts. According to Fanon, the French actions turned radio listening into a revolutionary act, transforming passive listeners into active participants. Fanon wrote:

> The listener, enrolled in the battle of the waves, had to figure out the tactics of the enemy and in an almost physical way circumvent the strategy of the adversary. Very often only the operator, his ear glued to the receiver, had the unhoped-for opportunity for hearing "the Voice." The other Algerians present in the room would receive the echo of this voice through the privileged interpreter who, at the end of the broadcast, was literally besieged. Specific questions would then be asked of this reincarnated voice. . . . A real task of reconstruction would then begin. Everyone would participate.[12]

The process of listening to the broadcasts, circumventing the jamming, and reconstructing what was said turned every Algerian into a participant in the revolution.

Other free radio stations appeared in the Middle East during 1958, denouncing U.S. military intervention in Lebanon and British intervention in Jordan. The free stations had such names as the Voice of Free Lebanon, Voice of the People, and Voice of Arabism. A few years later, backers of deposed Iranian leader Mossadegh, who was ousted in a CIA-inspired coup, started a free station called the Free Voice of Iran that criticized Shah Mohammed Reza Pahlavi and his U.S. backers.

The African Independence Party of Guinea-Bissau and the Cape Verde Islands (PAIGC), founded in 1956 to oust Portuguese colonialism, started the first free radio station in sub-Saharan Africa. The PAIGC acquired a powerful shortwave transmitter in 1967, which it used for instruction, education, and "for special programs aimed at Portuguese troops."[13] The programs directed at Portuguese troops apparently had some impact; Portuguese troops revolted in 1974, ousting the dictatorship of Marcello Caetano in Portugal and ending the long-running national liberation wars in Portugal's colonies.

Since then, free radio stations have appeared in numerous African countries. In Ethiopia, the Tigre People's Liberation Front and Eritrean People's Liberation Front operated free stations during their long, successful battle to oust the Mengistu dictatorship. In south Sudan, the Sudan People's Liberation Army (SPLA) operates a free station that opposes the Muslim-dominated government in the north, which it has been fighting since 1983. And in Nigeria, democratic opponents of the military dictatorship operate several free radio stations—Radio Democrat International, Radio Kudirat Nigeria, and the Voice of Free Nigeria.[14]

Free radio stations have also appeared throughout Latin America. In Cuba, opponents of dictator Fulgencio Batista operated numerous free stations. The best known of these was *Radio Rebelde,* operated by Fidel Castro's rebel army starting in February 1958 from their base camp in the Sierra Maestra mountains.

The idea for Radio Rebelde came from Che Guevara, who believed that a free radio station was needed to reach supporters outside of the guerrilla zone. Radio was able to reach everyone in Cuba and to stir their emotions, something that newspapers could not do. In *Guerrilla Warfare,* Guevara wrote, "The radio is a factor of extraordinary importance. At moments when war fever is more or less palpitating in a region or a country, the inspiring, burning word increases this fever and communicates it to every one of the future combatants. It explains, teaches, fires, and fixes the future positions of both friends and enemies."

According to Guevara, radio could be used to reach city dwellers, whom the rebels could recruit to their cause. Not only would listeners become sympathetic to the cause, but the radio station could provide them within instructions on how to become guerrillas. "All problems should be discussed by radio—for example, the way to defend oneself from air attacks, and the location of enemy forces," Guevara wrote.[15]

Che Guevara's ideas of guerrilla warfare inspired several generations of Latin Americans, and continue to serve as an inspiration to many. In Latin America today, several guerrilla armies operate, and almost every one of them has a free radio station. In Colombia, the Rebel Armed Forces (FARC) operates *La Voz de Resistencia* and the National Liberation Army (ELN) operates *Radio Patria Libre,* which government troops have repeatedly attempted to silence.[16] In Guatemala, *La Voz Popular* is operated by the National Liberation Unity (UNRG) "from the mountains of the Sierra Madre." In December 1996 the UNRG signed an agreement with the Guatemalan government, formally ending the country's civil war. And in Mexico, the Zapatista National Liberation Army operates a free station from its jungle base in Chiapas.[17]

Free stations have even appeared in urban areas of Latin America. In Brazil, where most legal stations are owned by corporations and wealthy individuals (as is the case in the United States) free broadcasting stations have appeared. The free stations discuss issues that the legal stations refuse to address, such as the police-run assassination teams that murder homeless people, the terror directed at environmental and Indian activists by large landowners and their allies in provincial governments, and the huge income gap between Brazil's rich and poor. By 1996 several hundred free radio stations operated in São Paulo alone. The sheer number of these stations has forced the government to consider changing its broadcasting laws to allow these low-power stations to operate legally.[18]

Although most free stations in the post–World War II era have broadcast to Third World countries with repressive, authoritarian governments, free radio stations have also operated in Western Europe. In France, Belgium, and Italy, free stations have appeared in an effort to circumvent centralized, government-controlled broadcasting.

Free Radio in France

Between the end of World War II and the 1981 election of Socialist president Francois Mitterrand, French radio and television broadcasting was centrally and politically controlled. Radio France, controlled by a succession of government agencies such the ORTF (*Office de Radiodiffusion-television francaise*), operated the county's radio networks, which competed with a group of peripheral commercial stations broadcasting from border regions. The main peripheral stations—Radio Monte Carlo, Sud Radio (based in Andorra), and Europe No. 1 (based in West Germany)—were also controlled by the French government through the *Societe Financiere de Radiodiffusion*, which owned or partly owned these stations.

Although the conservative governments that ruled France until 1981 claimed that Radio France operated in a nonpartisan manner, French radio was clearly the mouthpiece of government. It provided the government's version of the Algerian war to the French public, refused to discuss the prejudice against North Africans who came to France after the FLN victory, and provided government leaders with access and coverage while denying it to the political opposition. For example, in 1964 President Charles De Gaulle ordered French broadcasting to restrict coverage of the presidential election—but not of the French president—until two weeks before the election, giving him a massive election advantage.[19]

Even after broadcasting was supposedly reformed in 1975, access to the electronic media by minor party candidates was restricted, and political parties and unions were not given time to reply to attacks on them by journalists or government leaders. The entrenched parties also exerted pressure on ORTF to ensure that pro-government reporting predominated.

Failing to get equal access to the broadcast media, Communists, Socialists, Greens, and union activists decided that the only way to get their views heard was to set up their own illegal *radios libres*. The *Confédération Générale du Travail* (CGT), the Communist-led labor confederation, started *Radio Quinquin* in the northern city of Auby and *Radio Lorraine-Coeur d'Acier* ("Radio Heart of Steel") in the northeastern city of Nancy. In Alsace, near the border with Germany, Luxembourg, and Belgium, a collective of Green activists started *Radio Verte Fessenheim*, which was the first to freely address ecological issues, including the construction of nuclear power plants in the region. In Paris, the Greens operated Radio Verte Paris, and the Socialists operated Radio Riposte, which directly attacked the policies of French President Valéry Giscard d'Estaing.

In response, the government passed legislation in 1978 reaffirming its monopoly on broadcasting. The legislation warned free radio broadcasters that their stations were illegal and would be forcibly silenced if they did not voluntarily go off the air, which few did. After this, the government took often brutish action against the free radio broadcasters.

Police first started jamming the free stations but soon changed their tactics. On June 28, 1979, French police stormed the Parisian headquarters of the Socialist party, from which they believed Radio Riposte was broadcast. The police failed to locate the station, which resurfaced a few days later in the city of Montpellier. For making the illegal Radio Riposte broadcasts, the government indicted Socialist party leader Lurent Fabius, Senator Bernard Parmentier, and presidential candidate Francois Mitterrand, who announced over the station that he "came to defend a true cause: that of freedom of speech."[20] In France, the penalty for operating an illegal station was from one month to one year in jail or fines equivalent to between US$2,350 and US$23,500.

Mitterrand announced that the indictment was political and that the government was manipulating French media. He therefore demanded a political trial, saying, "They wanted a political trial, they shall have one." His defiance rallied free stations to his cause.[21]

As the presidential election approached in France, the government stepped up its attack on free radio. After closing the roads and cutting off electricity and telephone lines during the predawn hours of June 4, 1980, twelve companies of helmeted police stormed Radio Quinquin, bludgeoning supporters of the station who had gathered outside, breaking down the station's door, arresting the operators, and carting off the transmitter.

In Nancy, police attacked demonstrators before storming Radio Lorraine-Coeur d'Acier. In Paris, police raided Radio Paris 80, where they seized transmitters, turntables, and other broadcasting equipment. After the police left, the operators installed new equipment and were back on the air within hours, rallying supporters to assemble in front of the station. When police returned to the station later that day, they were confronted by several hundred protestors and quickly retreated.[22]

In 1981, in the midst of the presidential campaign, the police stormed Canal 75, which aired the views of opposition candidates in open defiance of government restrictions. Police raided the station and detained for four hours the station's operators and a bystander, whom the police threatened, saying next time they "would crack heads."[23]

Despite the intimidation, Mitterrand won the presidential election, promising to reform the French broadcasting system, which he sought to do almost immediately. After taking office, Mitterrand stopped the police raids and jamming of free radio stations and presented legislation legalizing low-power (500 watts or less) noncommercial FM stations, which the National Assembly soon passed. The legislation created a new agency, the *Haute Autorite,* to license and regulate the stations, because several hundred had already taken to the air.

Because of the large number of stations, several stations in Paris had to share the same frequency, rotating the hours during which they broadcast. Nevertheless, over 100 groups were assigned to twenty-two frequencies. Stations programming in Portuguese, Italian, Greek, and Armenian were asked to share the same frequency. Another frequency was assigned to Protestant and Catholic churches, which shared their frequency with the Boy Scouts. Gay groups, anarchists, feminists, environmentalists, Communists, Socialists, and even Gaullist groups applied for and received licenses, presenting French listeners with an array of new voices, many of which were not heard previously on French Radio.[24]

The Lessons of Free Radio

In each case described above, the free radio operations were adopted to the conditions existing in each country. In 1956 the Hungarian free radio stations broadcast from powerful aboveground transmitters that were seized by rebel groups. At the time, the electronic components needed to build smaller, portable transmitters were simply not available. As a consequence, these free stations were easily located by Soviet troops and silenced.

A dozen years later, when Soviet troops invaded Czechoslovakia, Czech and Slovak opponents of the invasion operated free stations, but they had learned from the Hungarian experience. The Czechoslovak free broadcasts were taped rather than made live, making it more difficult for the occupation troops to locate the studios and make arrests. The stations broadcast for short periods of time from government-owned auxiliary transmitters, rather than from the main transmitters of existing stations. This made it more difficult for the occupation troops to locate and silence the stations than in Hungary.

In Poland, following the declaration of martial law in 1981, members of the outlawed Solidarity labor union also made free radio broadcasts. Since a crackdown was anticipated and electronic components were cheap and widely available, Solidarity members constructed numerous inexpensive portable transmitters, which broadcast intermittently. These were very difficult for the authorities to locate. More powerful transmitters were placed in unfinished, high-rise apartment buildings in Warsaw, where electrical power was available and antennas could be placed high above the city, improving reception and increasing transmission distance. These transmitters were attached to tape recorders and timers. At predetermined times—which the public would learn from leaflets, chalk messages on sidewalks, and word-of-mouth—the hidden transmitters would go on the air, denouncing military rule. When the Polish police located the transmitters using tracking equipment, the only thing they found was the abandoned equipment; the station's operators were nowhere to be found, having set up the equipment hours earlier and then vanished.

In Chile, during the era of General Augusto Pinochet's military dictatorship when government-sponsored torture and murder were common, members of the Movement of the Revolutionary Left (MIR), a banned political group, operated free stations in a manner similar to Solidarity, but with an important twist—the transmitters were not only attached to timers, but were booby-trapped. When soldiers located a transmitter and stormed the transmission site, the equipment exploded. After some were killed in this manner, soldiers were reluctant to storm transmission sites, allowing the free radio stations to remain on the air for a longer period of time than they otherwise would have. In Chile, opponents of the military regime also operated micropower stations that broadcast to specific neighborhoods in Santiago. Because the stations broadcast with low power to limited geographic areas, they were not easily detected. Similar low-power neighborhood stations broadcast in Brazil during the period of military rule there.

In contrast to Europe and South America, where free radio stations often broadcast on the mediumwave (AM) and very high frequency (FM) bands, free radio stations in Africa usually broadcast on shortwave from transmitters located in guerrilla-controlled zones remote from urban areas or from foreign, but politically-sympathetic, countries. For example, the Popular Front for the Liberation of Sanguiet el Hamra and Rio de Oro (POLISARIO) broadcast to the Morocco-occupied Sahara over the Voice of Free Sahara for many years from transmitters based in or near Algeria. The use of shortwave rather than mediumwave transmitters made it difficult for Morocco to determine their exact location because shortwave transmissions bounce off the ionosphere and then back to earth before being received. By contrast, AM and FM stations transmit ground waves, which can be triangulated, making it easy to locate their transmitters. Thus it is less likely that free radio broadcasters operating on shortwave will be located and their transmitters seized or bombed.

Moreover, when free radio broadcasters transmit on the shortwave band, they can locate their transmitters a great distance from the regions to which they broadcast. Free radio broadcasters can locate their transmitters in a remote, guerrilla-controlled zone or even in distant country and still be capable of broadcasting throughout the target country. Of course, free radio broadcasts on shortwave make sense only when shortwave receivers are common in a country, which is not the situation in the United States and many other countries. In the United States, free radio stations need to broadcast on FM, the most widely listened-to band, to reach listeners. Broadcasting on shortwave would be futile.

NOTES

1. *The World Almanac and Book of Facts for 1935* (New York: New York World-Telegram, 1935), p. 389; *The World Almanac and Book of Facts for 1950* (New York: New York World-Telegram, 1950), p. 755.

2. David Close, "The Reconstruction of A Right-Wing State," in *The Greek Civil War, 1943–1950*, ed. David Close (New York: Routledge, 1993), pp. 156–189; David Close, *The Origins of the Greek Civil War* (New York: Longman, 1995), pp. 150–188.

3. Donald Browne, "The Voice of Palestine: A Broadcasting House Divided," *Middle East Journal* 29 (1975): 133–150.

4. Charles Ameringer, *The Democratic Left in Exile* (Coral Gables, Fla.: University of Miami Press, 1974), p. 41.

5. Charles Ameringer, *The Caribbean Legion* (University Park, Pa.: The Pennsylvania State University Press, 1996), p. 72.

6. Ameringer, *The Democratic Left in Exile*, p. 77.

7. According to M. C. Ricklefs, the "Japanese finally made a public announcement of their surrender" on August 22. However, the Japanese did not announce that Indonesia had declared its independence. M. C. Ricklefs, *A History of Modern Indonesia* (Bloomington, Ind.: Indiana University Press, 1981), p. 202.

8. Robert Cribb, *Gangsters and Revolutionaries* (Honolulu: University of Hawaii Press, 1991), p. 61; Lawrence Soley, "The Clandestine Radio Connection," *Stamps*, June 13, 1987, p. 36.

9. Robert Cribb and Colin Brown, *Modern Indonesia* (New York: Longman, 1995), p. 21.

10. Sheila O'Brien, "East Asia: Where the Spectrum Is Dark," in *Clandestine Radio Broadcasting*, ed. Lawrence Soley and John Nichols (New York: Praeger, 1987), pp. 257–258, 294.

11. Frantz Fanon, *Studies in a Dying Colonialism* (New York: Monthly Review Press, 1965), p. 74.

12. Ibid., p. 85.

13. Basil Davidson, *The Liberation of Guiné* (Baltimore: Penguin, 1969), p. 127.

14. Monica Downer, "Clandestine Radio in African Liberation Movements: A Study of the Eritrean Struggle for Self-Determination," *Communication Inquiry* 17(1993): 93–104; British Broadcasting Corporation, "Nigerian Opposition Radio Interrupted by London's WRN," *Summary of World Broadcasts*, June 20, 1996, p. EE/0025.

15. Che Guevara, *Guerrilla Warfare* (New York: Monthly Review Press, 1961), pp. 98–99.

16. "More than 50 Servicemen, Guerrillas Killed in Colombian Battle," Reuters, December 12, 1990; "Police Discover Clandestine Radio Station," *Foreign Broadcasting Information Service Daily Report* (LAT) January 4, 1989, p. 30.

17. Gregory Katz and Tracey Eaton, "Mexican Rebels Reject Peace Terms," *Dallas Morning News*, January 6, 1994, p. 1A; Peter Eisner, "Critics Say Mexican Government Mishandled Unrest," *Newsday*, January 12, 1994, p. 13.

18. British Broadcasting Corporation, "Pirate Radios," *Summary of World Broadcasts*, March 14, 1996, p. EE/0011.

19. For a more extensive discussion of French governmental control of broadcasting, see Donald Browne, *Comparing Broadcast Systems* (Ames, Iowa: Iowa State University Press, 1989), pp. 71–83.

20. Reuters, "International News," November 18, 1981, BC cycle.

21. "Pirate Politics," *Economist*, September 1, 1979, p. 21; "French Socialist Leader Charged for Clandestine Radio Broadcasts," *Washington Post*, August 24, 1979, p. A18.

22. Edward Girardet, "Sparks Fly as French Pull Plug on Pirate Radio Stations," *Christian Science Monitor*, June 17, 1980, p. 5.

23. "French Pirate Radio Station to Try Again," United Press International, March 11, 1981, AM cycle.

24. "French Radio; Freedom Without Commercials," *Economist*, September 3, 1983, p. 4; David White, "Bitter Battle in France for the 'Freedom of the Air,'" *Financial Times*, April 1, 1982, p. 2. Under pressure form commercial broadcasters such as Radio NRJ, which vio-

lated the government's restrictions on power and advertising, the broadcasting law was changed in 1984, permitting stations to sell advertising. The change forced many community stations off the air, since they could not financially compete with the commercial stations. Many of the licenses of community stations have since been taken over by commercial stations, thus reducing the array of views expressed on French radio. See Jean-Paul Lafrance and Jean Paul Simon, "France: Broadcasting in Turmoil," in *The People's Voice*, ed. Nick Jankowski et al. (London: John Libbey, 1992), pp. 176–179.

4

Limits on Free Speech
in the United States:
Government Licensing and
Corporate Censorship

In nations where governments directly censor the mass media, as in present-day Nigeria, the functions of free radio are obvious to the government, the station's operators, its listeners, and even foreign observers. Free radio is the safest, least expensive, and least labor intensive method for circumventing government restrictions on free expression, which is why repressive governments jam, bomb, and otherwise try to silence free radio stations and harass, arrest, and sometimes execute those who operate them.

In liberal democracies such as France, where the government owned and controlled broadcasting stations until 1981, the functions of free radio are also obvious. Free radio was a method by which opposition voices disseminated their views while simultaneously demonstrating in a nonviolent way their opposition to the government's broadcasting policies.

In the United States, the need for free radio is less obvious, because government controls are indirect and media ownership, and consequently censorship, are private. Although not as obvious, the need for free radio stations is even greater in the United States than in places like pre-Mitterrand France, because the combination of indirect government control and corporate media ownership has produced impediments to free expression that are greater than anything that existed under Gaullist rule in France.

Although there are nearly 1,700 daily newspapers, 12,000 radio stations, and 1,500 television stations in the United States, far more than in any other country, the range of political and cultural views expressed by the U.S. media is far more restricted than in most other countries regarded as democracies. One reason for this is that the vast majority of newspapers and broadcasting stations are owned by corporate entities, which have a vested interest in the status quo. Over 85 percent of AM and FM radio stations are owned by for-profit corporations that control the licenses for the best broadcasting frequencies, such as clear channel AM stations.[1] In the United States there are fewer than 150 community radio stations, which allow members of the public to be involved in news and program production, and most of these are relegated to the noncommercial portion of the FM spectrum.

Moreover, the U.S. media depend primarily on government officials to define routine news, rely on a small group of former politicians and government officials to analyze and shape news events, and restrict their coverage of political candidates to those whom the media and political leaders consider to be mainstream. These limitations on reporting and access are euphemistically referred to as "gatekeeping" by the mass media, thus implying that the policies are not really censorship.[2]

By contrast, Poland, a former Communist state, has far more diversified media than the does the United States. Poland's largest circulation daily is *Gazeta Wyborcza*, founded by Solidarity members in 1989. The second largest circulation daily is *Rzeczpospolita*, which is jointly owned by the Polish government and French media magnate Robert Hersant, and the largest circulation weekly is *Nie*, a pro-Communist newspaper owned by former Communist leader Jerzy Urban. Similar diversity is found in the broadcast media, where public television and radio stations effectively compete with commercial stations. As a result, Polish "opinion polls show that the public has more confidence in the media than in most of the country's political institutions."[3]

In the United States, the public has a very different attitude toward the media—and rightly so. About two-thirds of respondents to a *Los Angeles Times* poll thought that "the press looks out mainly for powerful people," and nearly 70 percent agreed that "the news media give more coverage to stories that support their own point of view than to those that don't."[4]

The Government-Granted Monopoly

During World War I, all radio transmissions in the United States were controlled by the U.S. Navy, which viewed the air waves as a strategic resource for fighting the Central Powers. Transmitters and receivers were used to coordinate air raids and ship movements, detect enemy submarines, decode enemy messages, and execute trench warfare, which relied on aerial reconnaissance and "trench transmitters."[5]

In the years immediately following World War I, the federal government, with little public debate or involvement, stripped the navy of its power and turned broadcasting over to one commercial firm, the Radio Corporation of America (RCA). The rationale for allowing a single company to control radio broadcasting technologies—technologies that the company had not developed—was that radio was a natural monopoly of such strategic importance that it needed to be controlled by a U.S.-based corporation, rather than a foreign entity. With the assistance of federal officials, RCA—controlled by the General Electric Corporation (GE), American Telephone & Telegraph (AT&T), and the Westinghouse Corporation—forced the British-owned Marconi Company to transfer its patents and assets to the American-based corporation in 1919, thus creating a monopoly. According to Erik Barnouw, author of a highly regarded history of American broadcasting, "Under the GE-RCA-AT&T-Westinghouse agreements, an effort had been made to allocate everything. The making of receivers and parts would be done by GE and Westinghouse; the marketing of these receivers would be done through RCA. . . . The sale of transmitters would be mainly an AT&T concern."[6] In effect, the RCA companies were given complete control over broadcasting, except when it concerned "amateur" broadcasting, which the patent agreements excluded.

Although the RCA companies started radio stations, it was the amateur stations that actually created the AM broadcasting boom of the early 1920s. The RCA companies did not believe that broadcasting was profitable, so they encouraged "amateurs" to build and operate radio stations using RCA-patented equipment. The greater the number of stations on the air, Westinghouse and GE concluded, the greater the demand for their receivers, and the more receivers they sold, the greater their profits.

Amateur stations were started by educational institutions, churches, department stores, and even a labor union—the Chicago Federation of Labor (CFL). All had different motivations for going on the air. For example, the motivation of colleges and universities was to broadcast home study courses for students and agricultural news for farmers. By the end of 1924, over 100 university stations were broadcasting.

After RCA realized that profits could be made from the sale of radio advertising, the corporation, which had the ear of key federal officials and legislators, lobbied the government to limit the number of broadcasting stations on the air. RCA maintained that "a limited group of 'superpower' stations strategically located to serve the entire country" were all that the country needed. The hoped-for superpower stations, of course, were to be operated by the RCA companies. In response to this lobbying, Secretary of Commerce Herbert Hoover, who granted licenses for radio broadcasting, authorized RCA-Westinghouse's WJZ and General Electric's WGY to boost their power to 50,000 watts. In 1924 and 1925, Hoover followed the advice of the RCA group and stopped issuing licenses for new stations and changed the frequencies and times that other stations were allowed to broadcast.[7] Hoover's decisions were challenged in federal court and overturned.

The court ruled that Hoover lacked authority to stop issuing licenses or to restrict the hours that stations could broadcast.[8] Following the court decision, over one hundred new stations went on the air, and many existing stations increased their wattage and hours of operation.

Government Censorship Through Licensing

In response to industry lobbying, interference on AM frequencies, and the federal court decision, Congress passed the Radio Act of 1927, creating the Federal Radio Commission (FRC). Among other things, the commission was to license radio stations "if public convenience, interest or necessity is thereby served." The Act stipulated that broadcast licenses be issued for three-year, renewable intervals and that the air waves remain the property of the United States government.[9]

The new radio commission, appointed by Republican president Calvin Coolidge, demonstrated that it defined "public convenience, interest and necessity" as commercial broadcasting: Rather than looking at a station's programming to determine whether it merited a license, the FRC chose to look at technical factors where commercial stations were strongest and noncommercial stations were weakest, such as the quality of transmitters. In choosing this criterion, the FRC assured that noncommercial stations would lose their assignments, thus giving commercial voices an oligopoly—if not a monopoly—over broadcasting.

To assure that commercial voices would dominate the airwaves, the FRC also utilized rhetorical deceptions, many of which are still commonly used today.[10] For example, the commission defined noncommercial stations operated by educational institutions, unions, and religious orders as "special interest" or "propaganda" stations, which it contrasted with "general public service" stations. The FRC defined "propaganda" stations as those attempting to spread a particular viewpoint or those interested in reaching members of their group, not all potential listeners. The FRC looked on these stations with disfavor, stating that "there is not room in the broadcast band for every school of thought, religious, political, social or economic." In contrast, commercial broadcasters sought to reach the largest possible audiences with their messages, so that they could charge advertisers more for advertising time. Because they sought to maximize their audiences, commercial broadcasters were called "general public service" broadcasters and were therefore given licensing priority.[11] Through the use of this rhetorical device, the FRC was able to shut down or drastically reduce the operating hours of noncommercial stations.

At the same time that the FRC was forcing noncommercial stations off the air, it was assigning the best frequencies to commercial stations: Twenty-one of the twenty-four clear channels created by the FRC were assigned to stations affiliated with RCA's National Broadcasting Corporation (NBC) network or the newly formed Columbia Broadcasting System (CBS) network. The FRC also relied heavily upon commercial broadcast engineers for advice on frequency assignments.[12]

University-operated radio stations were badly injured by the FRC's actions. Many were forced to operate during daytime only, when nontraditional students, whom the stations were trying to reach, were at work. Others were forced from the air. In *A Tower in Babel* Erik Barnouw describes what happened to Nebraska Wesleyan University's pioneering station, WCAJ:

> In 1927 the FRC assigned it to 860 kc; then moved it to 790, sharing with KMMJ; then, in 1928, to 590, sharing with WOW, Omaha, which was given six-sevenths of the time. . . . WOW applied to the FRC for the full-time; when this was denied, appealed to the District of Columbia Court of Appeals. . . . Each such hearing meant legal and travel costs for the Nebraska Wesleyan station . . . Eventually, worn down by litigation, hearings and travel costs, the University station sold out—to WOW. A number of case histories followed this sequence.[13]

By 1937 only 38 educational stations remained on the air. The religious, social service and labor stations were also forced off the air.[14]

By 1934, the year Congress passed the Communications Act, replacing the FRC with the Federal Communications Commission (FCC), noncommercial radio broadcasting in the United States had been eviscerated and opponents of corporate control were effectively barred from the air waves. The most powerful stations were network affiliates, which were unwilling to air views that challenged their supremacy of the airwaves.

The newly formed FCC continued the practices instituted by the FRC. Congress, alarmed by the FRC's gutting of noncommercial broadcasting, required the FCC to study and report back to Congress on possibility of assigning "fixed percentages of radio broadcasting facilities to particular types or kinds of nonprofit radio programs or to persons identified with particular kinds of nonprofit activities." In 1935 the FCC reported to Congress that existing commercial stations provided ample educational programming and that no special frequencies needed to be assigned for noncommercial purposes.[15]

There are several reasons why the FCC, like its predecessor, produces regulations benefitting corporate broadcasters. First, FCC commissioners usually have come from telecommunications industries—the very industries that the FCC is supposed to police.[16] Second, commissioners who prove to be loyal supporters of corporate interests are rewarded with high-paying industry jobs after leaving the FCC. Consumer activists like Ralph Nader have referred to this as "deferred bribery." A study of FCC commissioners who served between 1945 and 1970 found that twenty-one of the thirty-three commissioners became employees of, lobbyists for, or lawyers representing the telecommunications industry after leaving the commission. The other twelve commissioners were elderly and retired upon leaving their FCC posts.[17]

Third, commercial broadcasters, through trade associations such as the National Association of Broadcasters (NAB), maintain a constant lobbying presence in Washington by testifying at hearings that affect their interests and cultivating personal contacts with politicians, commissioners, and other power brokers. Broadcasters are also some of the biggest contributors to the Democratic and Republican parties, assuring that politicians from both parties are indebted to them.[18]

Fourth, corporate media owners use all of their resources—including the mass media and politicians in their debt—to ensure that the FCC and other regulators adopt rules favoring their interests. Corporate media slant news and editorialize in favor of regulations that help them, and they publicly attack regulations that restrict their power, influence, and profits.[19] Broadcasting corporations can do this with impunity because the FCC revoked the Fairness Doctrine in 1987.[20] This doctrine, originally adopted because of Congressional pressure on the FCC, stated that broadcasting stations must provide the public with "a reasonable opportunity to hear different opposing positions on the public issues of interest and importance in the community."[21] It required broadcasting stations to give free reply time to opponents of their editorial positions. The revocation of the Fairness Doctrine has allowed broadcasting corporations to present highly biased, one-sided presentations of issues.

In addition to slanting stories, corporate media black out stories about laws and regulations that directly effect them, thus denying citizens knowledge of the legislative and regulatory process and reducing their involvement in it. The least covered story of 1995, according to Sonoma State University's "Project Censored," was the Telecommunication Deregulation Bill, which eliminated FCC limits on the number of AM, FM, and television stations that a corporation can own.[22] The bill, which Congress passed with little public debate, opened the door to increased concentration in the industry, including Westinghouse Corporation's takeover of CBS and Disney's takeover of ABC.

FM Broadcasting

A history of radio broadcasting on the FM bandwidth, where most U.S.-based free stations broadcast, provides a clear picture of how the FCC and its licensing process has furthered the interests of corporate broadcasters. The FCC first tried to stifle FM broadcasting, despite its technical superiority to AM broadcasting, because corporate broadcasters like RCA were content with their domination of AM and were unwilling to invest in FM stations. By stifling FM's development, the FCC assured that AM broadcasting would not face competition from a new medium.

When the FCC finally opened up FM, it gave FM licenses to the companies controlling AM radio, thus inhibiting the growth of the new medium. And after FM became popular with listeners, the FCC banned low-power, noncommercial FM stations, eliminating one of the few areas of broadcasting that corporations did not dominate.

FM broadcasting was invented in the 1930s by Edwin Armstrong, but FCC policies inhibited its growth for decades. First, the FCC did not allocate spectrum space for FM broadcasting until just before World War II started. When the war ended, the FCC reviewed its prewar spectrum allocations and moved FM from channel one to right above television channel six, at 88–108 MHz. The FCC decision made existing FM receivers obsolete "and set the medium back for years. The RCA-NBC forces . . . rejoiced." The FCC decision protected "the status quo in radio while providing spectrum space for the expansion of television."[23]

Despite the setback for FM, many AM broadcasters nevertheless sought insurance against the growth of FM by requesting and getting FM licenses. Rather than helping the medium develop, these broadcasters merely *simulcast*, that is, transmitted the same programming on FM as AM, thus reducing the incentive for consumers to listen to FM. Moreover, simulcasting badly hurt independent FM broadcasters, who could not compete with AM for advertising support because advertisers flocked to where large numbers of listeners could be found—which was on AM. As a consequence, FM broadcasting languished for nearly twenty years.

Because of the FCC's decision, FM remained unprofitable. The number of operating FM stations on the air declined between 1950 and 1956, dropping from 676 to 534 stations. Most of the stations that signed off had been operated by independent FM broadcasters, not simulcasters. Receiver sales also dropped, falling from 2.2 million sets sold in 1950 to less than a quarter million in 1956.[24]

To make their decision to move FM more publicly palatable, the FCC reserved frequencies between 88 and 92 MHz for educational, noncommercial broadcasting. At the time, these frequencies had little commercial value. Nevertheless, because the decision provided them with access to the airwaves, colleges and universities expressed their support for the FCC's decision, even though it meant that universities would be broadcasting on channels that few people could receive.

Few universities and nonprofit groups had the money to build and operate full-power FM stations, so the FCC relaxed its rules in 1948, permitting noncommercial stations to operate with low power (10 watts). After low-power broadcasting was approved, the number of noncommercial FM stations increased steadily during the 1950s and 1960s.[25]

FM did not blossom until the late 1960s, when the "underground music" format became popular among college-age youths rebelling against the crass commercialism of AM radio, which selectively aired music on the basis of lyrics and length. The corporate-owned AM stations would not air recordings that had controversial political lyrics or were longer than three minutes.

Former AM disc jockey Tom Donahue believed that a large audience existed for counterculture recordings and contacted KMPX-FM in San Francisco, a nearly bankrupt independent station carrying foreign language programs, to ask whether the station would consider changing its format. The station did change,

Donahue was named program director, and "underground" FM was born. KMPX minimized deejay chat, refused jingle-based commercials, played the recordings that AM stations wouldn't, and dedicated itself to the counterculture, decorating its studio with tapestries, Vietcong flags, and black light posters.[26]

KMPX's success was quickly copied by several independent commercial stations and noncommercial college stations. After these stations demonstrated the popularity of the underground or "progressive rock" format, as it was also called, FM stations owned by corporate giants such as ABC, RKO, and Westinghouse also adopted—and coopted—the format. The corporate giants used their deep pockets to lure well-known deejays away from independent FM stations and used their marketing muscle to get and air new recordings by popular artists before other stations. This assured them of larger audiences and hence greater profitability than that garnered by the other stations.

The corporate stations soon cracked down on political and social advocacy by deejays. Some deejays were sacked for making controversial statements about politicians and advertisers; others were silenced with threats of firing. The new attitude was summed up by a poster on the wall of one commercial FM station: "The Age of Aquarius is over—and now it's time to kick ass."[27]

By the late 1970s, the corporate-owned stations, which had begun to dominate the format, were again discriminating against recording artists. Punk rock and new wave bands like The Dead Kennedys and the Runaways, whose songs were filled with discomforting beats and controversial lyrics, could not get aired on commercial FM stations, which filled the airwaves with music from cliché-slinging crooners like Kiss, AC/DC, and Supertramp. It was noncommercial stations, particularly college radio stations, that rescued new wave music from the commercial blackout.[28] Stations like the University of Georgia's WUOG aired not only recordings by better-known bands like the Clash, but also recordings by little-known, local bands like REM and Pylon that, as a result, acquired national reputations.

The Rise and Fall of Noncommercial FM

After the FCC reserved 88–92 MHz for noncommercial FM and permitted low-power FM broadcasting, three types of noncommercial radio stations evolved. The first and largest consisted of college and university radio stations. By 1969 when FM broadcasting began to emerge from two decades of stagnation, there were 384 of these stations on the air, the majority operating with low power.[29]

Another type of noncommercial operation was the community radio station, which was dedicated to airing views not heard over commercial stations. Community radio began in 1949 when the Pacifica Foundation received a license to operate KPFA in Berkeley—the first noncommercial license that didn't go to an educational institution. The premise under which KPFA was founded is that radio "should not be run by entrepreneurs motivated by profit, but by journalists and artists, whose motive would be the most objective and enlightening programming possible."[30] The Pacifica Foundation subsequently started stations in Los Angeles, New York, Washington, D.C., and Houston.

Pacifica's stations serve their communities through a local advisory board, which approves the station's budget, suggests programming, and provides two members to the Foundation's national advisory board. The national board advises Pacifica's national executive director, who hires and fires each station's general manager.

Although advised by community members, Pacifica stations are not owned or controlled by the community, and over the years this has produced conflicts—between community groups and Pacifica's executive directors and between local employees and station management. One of these conflicts erupted in 1993 after Pacifica's executive director decided to produce more national programming, which meant that Pacifica needed funding from national sources, such as foundations, in addition to listener support and that stations would be cutting back on local programming. This led to programming shakeups, which fueled protests that Pacifica was changing its programming to curry favor with foundations. In Berkeley, a "Save KPFA" committee was formed to protest the changes; Pacifica was getting "more mainstream," complained Curt Gray, a member of Save KPFA.

Marci Lockwood, KPFA's acting general manager during the protests, disagreed that the station was becoming mainstream, yet offered the following explanations for the changes at KPFA: "Now we have this perceived friend in the White House. We don't have Reagan or Bush. The Soviet Union is no longer an enemy. It's time for us to reevaluate what we're doing." Part of this reevaluation included getting rid of volunteer programmers who came to the station during the 1960s. "The issues they're covering may not be as relevant in 1993 as 1963. . . . Once they're on they never get off. But the air time belongs to Pacifica. It's not your time to do whatever you want with," she said, explaining why she wanted to replace the long-time volunteers.[31]

Save KPFA protesters had a different view. They saw the station as having become "intertwined with Berkeley's Democratic party machine." According to these critics, KPFA refused to do "any real aggressive community reporting and investigative news," had a "hands-off" policy toward Berkeley's liberal establishment, and even helped Berkeley's mayor and city manager hide their involvement in the building of volleyball courts in People's Park, the symbol of radical activism since the '60s. (The volleyball courts touched off protests in 1991 that eventually cost nearly $1.3 million to quell.[32]) Dismissing KPFA's more radical programmers made it easier to pursue these relationships.

As an example of KPFA's collusion with the Democratic party machine, Stephen Dunifer, who founded Free Radio Berkeley partly in response to the changes at Pacifica (see Chapter 7), cited a live on-air interview conducted with Berkeley mayor Loni Hancock by KPFA staffer Dennis Bernstein. During the interview, Bernstein confronted Mayor Hancock with evidence that she had communicated with university officials about their plans to build the courts in People's Park, which she had previously denied, and that she had discussed security actions that might be taken in the event of protests. After the interview, KPFA management sent Bernstein word to "lay off the Mayor." KPFA listeners were never informed of this because of a station gag rule prohibiting staffers from discussing internal station matters on the air.[33]

A different type of community radio station—one that was truly controlled and operated by local communities—was developed by Lorenzo Milam, who had worked at KPFA in the late 1950s and early 1960s. Milam founded Seattle's KRAB in 1964 as a model of community participation. In his view, community stations needed to "squeeze some of the art back into radio . . . for the poor and dispossessed to get back on the air, to have a chance to speak and be heard outside the next room, the next block."[34] This is what KRAB and subsequent community stations in Portland, St. Louis, Dallas, and Madison attempted to do. These and other community stations banded together to promote community radio through the National Federation of Community Broadcasters.

Unfortunately, the growth of community radio was stifled by the passage of the Public Broadcasting Act of 1967, which established the Corporation for Public Broadcasting (CPB) and National Public Radio (NPR). These quasi-governmental agencies promote and fund a different kind of noncommercial radio station—stations that are the antithesis of community radio—centralized, nationally oriented, and highly professional. To qualify as an affiliate of National Public Radio and receive federal funding, noncommercial stations have to meet CPB's standards: Stations have to operate a minimum of eighteen hours a day, disqualifying many college and community stations; to maintain at least five full-time professionals on staff and have an annual operating budget of $80,000, thus eliminating stations with shoestring budgets that served the poor and disenfranchised; and have at least 3,000 watts of power, thus eliminating low-power stations. Only seventy-three stations qualified for federal funding in 1970; four-fifths of the noncommercial stations did not qualify.[35] The few stations that did qualify were principally owned-and-operated by state or local governments, such as WNYC in New York City.

To remedy its lack of affiliates, National Public Radio asked the FCC to shut down low-power noncommercial stations, thereby making room in the noncommercial band for high-powered FM stations that would meet its qualifications.[36] Never one to rule against the rich or powerful, the FCC dutifully rescinded its rules on low-power FM stations. However, rather than merely pulling the plug on these stations, the FCC gave low-power stations eighteen months to upgrade their facilities and broadcast at 100 watts or more. Stations unable to upgrade were to move into the commercial band, if spectrum space was available in that city, or shut down. However, the low-power stations that did find an available commercial frequency were not protected from interference by more powerful commercial stations, thus reducing their chances of ever operating viably.

Many of the low-power stations decided to upgrade and qualify as NPR affiliates. Because NPR demanded that staffs be professional, these stations virtually closed their microphones to the public. Most of the remaining low-power stations signed off, ending that chapter of low-power FM broadcasting and shutting the door on the growth of community radio in the United States.

In addition to this policy, the FCC has established many others that have acted as barriers to community radio. These include requiring community applicants to conduct engineering studies, to use expensive, FCC-approved equipment, and to be sufficiently financed to operate the station at a loss, all of which preclude most community groups from even seeking licenses. In *Broadcasting in America*, Sydney Head described the problem: "Hearings [to get licenses] usually cost a great deal of money . . . the applicant [must] pay for engineering and other consultants, preparing and duplicating elaborate exhibits, purchasing hearing transcripts, transport and maintenance of witnesses in Washington, and the like." Head concluded that "broadcasting has a high cost of entry, which places significant limits on the opportunities to own broadcasting stations."[37] Most of the high costs associated with starting a broadcasting station were imposed by the FCC at the urging of corporate broadcasters, which explains why free radio stations can get off the ground and on the air for just a few hundred dollars.

Commercial Stations and Private Censorship

The FCC maintains that the large number of commercial broadcasters on the air in the United States assures that a diversity of viewpoints will be publicly presented. For example, the FCC explained that it was repealing the Fairness Doctrine because "viewpoint diversity is fully served by the multiplicity of voices in the marketplace today."[38]

However, most research suggests that there is uniformity, rather than diversity, in the opinions presented by the corporate-owned and corporate-underwritten media. For example, the three network news shows, CNN, the MacNeil/Lehrer News Hour (now called "the NewsHour with Jim Lehrer"), National Public Radio's *Morning Edition* and *All Things Considered*, and daily newspapers all turn to the same think tank pundits for expert opinion and commentary, which shapes or frames the way viewers interpret events. The American Enterprise Institute, Brookings Institution, and a handful of other think tanks provide analysis and commentary for most of the major news stories that media cover.[39] In *Manufacturing Consent*, Edward Herman and Noam Chomsky observed that relying extensively on analysts from these think tanks assures that dissident views are kept out of the media.[40]

The media's reliance on these think tanks and other so-called official sources, such as government officials, police, and corporate spokespersons, functions as a *news filter*, maintaining uniformity in the views presented. Academic research studies have shown that nonofficial sources—such as representatives of labor, peace, religious, and community organizations—are rarely quoted by the media.[41]

Not only are representatives of labor and community groups rarely used as sources in news stories, but they are oftentimes not even permitted to buy advertising time from the commercial media to express their views. Because the Fairness Doctrine has been rescinded, broadcasting stations, like newspapers, can refuse to sell advertising time to groups or individuals holding views with which the corporate media do not agree. For example, television stations in Minneapolis-St. Paul, refused to sell commercial time to the Prairie Island Sioux community, who produced a commercial critical of Northern States Power Company's plan to store spent nuclear fuel rods on the island.[42] Radio station KRVN in Nebraska not only refused to play a commercial advocating vegetarianism produced by People for the Ethical Treatment of Animals, in which country singer k.d. lang appeared as a spokesperson, but banned lang's songs from the air. Another owner of eight radio stations in Kansas and Oklahoma joined the boycott.[43] In Detroit, radio stations refused to sell advertising time to the United Auto Workers, which was calling for a boycott of Hudson stores following the corporation's intimidation of union organizers.[44]

One explanation for the stations' refusals to sell advertising time to the United Auto Workers and the Prairie Island Sioux is that Hudson and Northern States Power are frequent advertisers, and the mass media refuse to carry programming or advertising that might offend their advertisers. Examples of media killing or altering stories to avoid antagonizing advertisers are widespread. In addition to killing stories out of fear that they might offend advertisers, the media frequently acquiesce to direct pressures from advertisers, who want programming to carry a certain spin.[45]

Advertisers do not only pressure broadcasting stations and newspapers to kill or alter stories; the acceptance of advertising requires the media to produce programming that is conducive to selling the advertised products. In the advertising industry, this is called "compatible editorial environment." As a leading textbook on advertising strategy noted, programming "may not be well-suited to an advertiser's message because the editorial environments of the vehicles under consideration are incompatible with the ad message."[46] In cases of incompatible editorial environment, advertisers boycott the programming or medium, forcing it to sign off or to cease production.[47]

Because of their reliance on advertising dollars and corporate underwriting, which is another form of advertising support, most commercial and public radio stations develop programming that is acceptable to their sponsors, which is why all speak in favor of or fail to criticize corporate capitalism. There is consequently a uniformity of views expressed by radio stations, contrary to the assertions of the FCC concerning viewpoint diversity.

Another factor assuring a uniformity of media viewpoints is that all commercial broadcasting stations, which comprise the vast majority of stations, are owned by corporations or wealthy individuals who have a vested interest in corporate capitalism. Of commercial stations, the most powerful are owned by very large corporations, which have grown even larger since Congress passed the 1995 Telecommunication Deregulation Bill. In radio, Westinghouse is one of the largest group owners. With the acquisition of American Radio Systems, Westinghouse owns 175 stations and the Westwood One radio network, the nation's largest radio programmer, which syndicates the G. Gordon Liddy and Don Imus talk shows. Spokespersons for corporate oligopolies, such as talk show host Don Imus, claim that this a small number. "There are 11,000 [commercial] radio stations around the country. . . . For there to be some kind of monolithic invasion, we'd have to be on thousands."[48]

But the number of stations owned by a single corporation is misleading, since it says little about the market size or reach of the stations. When market size and reach are considered, Westinghouse's power and influence are immense, because it owns very powerful stations in the nation's largest cities. In New York City, it owns seven stations capturing over 20 percent of the listening audience and over 37 percent of radio advertising dollars. In Chicago, it owns ten stations capturing nearly 20 percent of the audience. And in Dallas-Ft. Worth it owns ten stations capturing over a quarter of the audience. It also owns four or more stations with large percentages of the audience in Los Angeles, San Francisco, Washington, D.C., Boston, Detroit, Philadelphia, Baltimore, and Houston.[49]

In cities where Westinghouse does not have a radio broadcasting oligopoly, another corporation usually does. For example, the oligopolist in Cincinnati is Jacor Communications, which owns 131 radio stations nationwide.[50] In Cincinnati, Jacor owns four FM and two AM stations that control about 30 percent of the listening audience and about 60 percent of radio advertising dollars.

Corporations such as these, which make millions of dollars annually from their control of the publicly-owned air waves, have very strong incentives for keeping programs critical of their power and profits from reaching the public. This explains why these corporations air an endless stream of conservative programming featuring Rush Limbaugh, G. Gordon Liddy, Michael Reagan, Ken Hamblin, and the like, rather than presenting a diversity of views, some of which would necessarily be critical of corporate power.

Corporations limit the diversity of views expressed by the media in other ways as well. The first and most important is by hiring reporters and managers who have assimilated corporate values. Individuals who have assimilated these values and regard them as the norm are less likely to quote, interview, or take seriously those with other viewpoints, which are considered to be "deviant."

Most survey studies, even those conducted by right-wing analysts, have shown that journalists overwhelmingly hold a corporate world view. For example, a study conducted by several conservative researchers found that:

> most are anything but socialists. For example, they overwhelmingly reject the proposition that major corporations should be publicly owned. Only one in eight would

agree to public ownership of corporations, and two-thirds declare themselves strongly opposed. Moreover, they overwhelmingly support the idea that people with greater ability should earn higher wages than those with less ability. Most also believe that free enterprise gives workers a fair shake, and that some deregulation of business would serve the national interest.[51]

Despite these pro-corporate views, journalists overwhelmingly regard themselves as liberals and detached analysts of economic and political affairs.

Another method of limiting public debate is *screening,* one of the best kept secrets in radio broadcasting. Screening is asking callers to radio programs what they intend to say before allowing them on the air. Although representatives of talk radio claim that callers are screened to weed out "kooks and nuts," screening is often a political litmus test. As the *San Diego Union* noted, Rush Limbaugh "carefully screens his [calls] so that only those who avidly agree with him get through."[52] When dissident callers slip though the screen, they are ridiculed, not given an opportunity to respond, and then cut off.

Free Radio and Free Speech

The system of broadcasting in the United States is designed for the benefit of broadcasting corporations, not the public. Since the establishment of the FRC in 1927, government policy has consistently discriminated against noncommercial broadcasting in favor of commercial broadcasting. As a result of this discrimination, most radio and television stations are commercial—owned by corporations and operated in their interest. Only 15 percent of AM and FM radio stations are noncommercial, and most of these are affiliated with NPR, which has effectively kept the public from participating in program production. In effect, NPR has functioned as a government-funded barrier to real community broadcasting.

Moreover, recent changes in broadcasting laws and regulations, such as the Telecommunication Deregulation Act and the revocation of the Fairness Doctrine, have vastly increased media corporations' control of the air waves and their ability to restrict free speech and public debate. Since the FCC and Congress have demonstrated their commitment to corporate rather than public welfare, they cannot be counted on to protect the public from corporate censorship. If anything, Congress and the FCC have abetted and legalized corporate censorship, and as long as corporate censorship exits, speech is not free.

There are two ways that the air waves can be freed from corporate control. One is to seize corporate broadcasting stations in the same way that Hungarian revolutionaries seized and operated state-controlled stations during the 1956 revolt. The disadvantages of this are obvious: U.S. authorities will dislodge rebel broadcasters here as surely and as quickly as Soviet troops dislodged the rebels in Hungary. Once dislodged, the corporate media will portray the rebels as thugs and hooligans rather than freedom fighters, just as Soviet-controlled media portrayed the Hungarian rebels as fascists and counterrevolutionaries.

The other way is by establishing free radio stations. The advantages of free radio are many. First, free radio stations demonstrate that FCC policies are designed to advance the interests of corporate broadcasters, not the public. For example, free radio stations show that the financial qualifications the FCC imposes on prospective broadcasters—that broadcasters have massive amounts of money available to operate the station in the red for at least a year—are designed to ensure that only the rich receive licenses. The FCC claims that it imposes these financial qualifications because underfinanced radio stations are likely to shut down, squandering a scarce public resource.[53] Numerous free stations operating on shoestring budgets have been on the air for years, some for nearly a decade, demonstrating the fallacy of the FCC claim.

Second, free radio stations represent a form of nonviolent civil disobedience against discriminatory government policy. The disobedience is aimed directly at the policy, just as the 1950s and 1960s sit-ins at Southern diners were aimed directly at the Jim Crow laws forbidding African-Americans from eating with whites.

Third, free radio stations allow opponents of FCC and corporate censorship to deliver their messages directly to the public, circumventing the media's elaborate filtering system, which distorts the content of opposition political messages. The only other alternatives for circumventing the media's filters and distortions are word of mouth and print media, which are labor intensive and costly. Moreover, most states have laws that hamper word of mouth and newspaper distribution. For example, all but a handful of states claim that shopping malls are private property and therefore restrict public speech and newspaper distribution at these locations. By prohibiting speech and newspaper distribution at malls, where approximately 70 percent of the public shops in any week, governments and private corporations—which own malls—effectively restrict the dissemination of alternative political messages.[54]

Fourth, free radio stations are one of the few avenues available for community members to freely express their grievances against the governing and owning classes. In modern America, the town hall meeting is obsolete, and where town hall meetings do occur, they are most often used by incumbent politicians to drum up support for unpopular policies or stalled reelection campaigns. In contrast, free radio stations allow community members to publicly and even anonymously express their grievances, unencumbered by the daunting presence of political leaders and police.

Lastly, free radio stations are a community organizing tool. A free radio station can inform citizens about public hearings, boycotts, meetings, and protests—something that leaflets, word-of-mouth, or telephoning can also do, but much less efficiently. Free radio stations can reach hundreds or even thousands of people in seconds without almost no effort. To reach the same number of people, a telephone campaign would require massive amounts of labor, thus diverting scarce resources to unnecessary, labor-intensive tasks. Thus, by depriving community groups of access to the air waves, the FCC has inhibited the development of grassroots organizations, which are forced to spend time and effort on simple communication tasks that can easily be accomplished using radio.

By airing announcements and encouraging public participation in running the station, free radio stations can assist community groups while simultaneously exposing the anti-public policies of the FCC. Community groups that have used the resources of free radio stations can therefore be mobilized in support of policies demanding that the FCC stop serving the corporate interest and start serving the public interest.

NOTES

1. *Broadcasting and Cable Yearbook 1995* (New Providence, N.J.: R. R. Bowker, 1995), p. xxi.

2. Edward S. Herman and Noam Chomsky, *Manufacturing Consent* (New York: Pantheon, 1988); Lawrence Soley, *The News Shapers* (New York: Praeger, 1992); Jane Brown et al., "Invisible Power: Newspaper News Sources and the Limits of Diversity," *Journalism Quarterly* 64 (1987): 45–54; D. Charles Whitney et al. "Geographic and Source Biases in Network Television News, 1982–1984," *Journal of Broadcasting and Electronic Media* 33 (1989): 159–174; Daniel Hallin, "Sound Bite News: Television Coverage of Election, 1968–1988," *Journal of Communication* 42 (1992): 5–24.

3. "World Press Freedom Review: Poland," *IPI Report,* December 1994, p. 61; "World Press Freedom Review: Poland," *IPI Report,* December 1995, pp. 83–84.

4. David Shaw, "Media Credibility Sinking," *Dallas Morning News,* June 20, 1993, p. 1J; David Shaw, "Trust in Media on Decline," *Los Angeles Times,* March 31, 1993, p. A1.

5. House Committee on the Merchant Marine and Fisheries, *Testimony of Secretary of the Navy, Josephus Daniels, Government Control of Radio Communication: Hearings before the Committee on the Merchant Marine and Fisheries,* 65th Cong., 3rd sess., December 12–19, 1918 (Washington, D.C.: Government Printing Office, 1919), p. 11.

6. Erik Barnouw, *A Tower in Babel* (New York: Oxford University Press, 1966), p. 81. Westinghouse actually joined the RCA conglomerate in 1921, after it had acquired patents that RCA had failed to get in the Marconi deal. United Fruit Company was also brought into RCA at this time because it also controlled important patents.

7. Ibid., pp. 174, 178–180.

8. *U.S. v. Zenith Radio Corp.*, 12 F. 2d 614 (1926).

9. The Radio Act of 1927, Public Law 632, 69th Cong. (February 23, 1927), reprinted in *Documents of American Broadcasting,* ed. Frank Kahn (Englewood Cliffs, N.J.: Prentice-Hall, 1973), pp. 36–51.

10. In an example of the continued use of this rhetorical deception, President Reagan during the 1980s repeatedly referred to women, minorities, and unions as "special interest groups" while equating corporations with the public interest. For a discussion of this, see

Juan Williams, "Reagan Is the King of Special Interest Groups," *Washington Post*, April 1, 1984, p. C1.

11. Robert McChesney, *Telecommunications, Mass Media, and Democracy* (New York: Oxford University Press, 1993), pp. 27–28, 66–67.

12. Barnouw, *A Tower in Babel*, pp. 216–218. Robert McChesney provides a different set of numbers that makes the same point. McChesney reports that "of the first twenty-five stations set aside for clear channels by the FRC, twenty-three had been licensed to broadcasters affiliated with NBC." McChesney, *Telecommunications, Mass Media, and Democracy*, p. 20.

13. Barnouw, *A Tower in Babel*, p. 219.

14. McChesney, *Telecommunications, Mass Media, and Democracy*, pp. 72–75.

15. Sydney Head, *Broadcasting in America*, 2d. ed. (Boston: Houghton Mifflin, 1972), p. 181.

16. Barry Cole and Mal Oettinger, *Reluctant Regulators: The FCC and the Broadcast Audience* (Reading, Mass.: Addison-Wesley, 1978), p. 5.

17. Roger Noll, Merton Peck, and John McGowen, *Economic Aspects of Television Regulation* (Washington, D.C.: Brookings Institution, 1973), pp. 123–124.

18. Cole and Oettinger, *Reluctant Regulators*, p. 92.

19. For case studies of how media corporations slant news and editorialize to advance their own interests, see James Squires, *Read All About It!* (New York: Times Books, 1993), pp. 121–124; and August K. Gribbin, "When Press Protects Its Turf," *Newspaper Research Journal* 16: 138–147. Squires discusses how Chicago Tribune Corp. executives used the *Tribune* to influence cable television policy. Gribbin found that publishers distorted the content of a telecommunications bill that would have allowed telephone companies to compete with them for advertising.

20. "Fairness Doctrine Obligations of Broadcast Licensees," 63 *Radio Register* (P & F) 488; R. D. Hersey, Jr., "F.C.C. Voted Down Fairness Doctrine in a 4–0 Decision," *New York Times*, August 5, 1987, p. A1.

21. "In the Matter of Editorializing by Broadcast Licensee," 13 FCC 1246 (June 1, 1949), in Kahn, *Documents of American Broadcasting*, p. 392.

22. Carl Jensen and Project Censored, *Censored: The News That Didn't Make the News and Why* (New York: Seven Stories Press, 1996), pp. 50–53, 283–286.

23. Ibid., pp. 242–243.

24. Peter Fornatale and Joshua Mills, *Radio in the Television Age* (Woodstock, N.Y.: Overlook Press, 1980), p. 123.

25. Head, *Broadcasting in America*, pp. 166, 182–183.

26. Michael Keith, *Voices in the Purple Haze* (New York: Praeger, 1997).

27. Fornatale and Mills, *Radio in the Television Age*, p. 142.

28. June Sullivan, "College Stations: Cutting Edge of Rock," *Boston Globe*, November 30, 1990, p. 41; Edna Gunderson, "College Radio Explores Rock's Flip Side," *USA Today*, February 27, 1989, p. 5D.

29. Peter Lewis and Jerry Booth, *The Invisible Medium: Public, Commercial, and Community Radio* (Washington, D.C.: Howard University Press, 1990), p. 46.

30. John Downing, *Radical Media* (Boston: South End Press, 1984), p. 75.

31. Frances Dinkelspeil, "Radical to Regular: Berkeley's 'Voice of the Voiceless' Under Fire for Changing with the Times," *Chicago Tribune*, November 28, 1993, p. 4C.

32. April Lynch and Louis Freedberg, "Protests at People's Park Cost $1.3 Million," *San Francisco Chronicle*, March 26, 1992, p. A19.

33. Stephen Dunifer, in person interview by author, March 4, 1997. Mayor Hancock of Berkeley joined the Clinton administration in 1993 as regional representative to U.S. Department of Education Secretary Richard Riley. See Janet Wells, "Berkeley Mayor Lists Priorities of New Job," *San Francisco Chronicle*, January 14, 1994, p. A20.

34. Lorenzo Milam, *Sex and Broadcasting* (Saratoga, Calif.: Dildo Press, 1975).

35. Fornatale and Mills, *Radio in the Television Age*, pp. 175–176; Thomas Warnock, "Public Radio: The Next Ten Years," in *The Future of Public Broadcasting*, ed. Douglass Cater and Michael Nyhan (New York: Praeger, 1976), p. 60.

36. "Changes in the Rules Relating to Noncommercial Educational FM Broadcast Stations," *69 FCC 2d. 240* (June 7, 1978); *68 FCC 2d. 985* (June 19, 1978).

37. Head, *Broadcasting in America*, p. 398.

38. "Fairness Doctrine Obligations of Broadcast Licensee," 63 *Radio Register 2d* (P & F) 488.

39. Lawrence Soley, *The News Shapers* (New York: Praeger, 1982).

40. Edward Herman and Noam Chomsky, *Manufacturing Consent* (New York: Pantheon, 1988).

41. Montague Kern, Patricia Levering, and Ralph Levering, *The Kennedy Crises: The Press, The Presidency, and Foreign Policy* (Chapel Hill: University of North Carolina Press, 1983); D. Charles Whitney et al., "Geographic and Source Biases in Network Television News 1982–1984," *Journal of Broadcasting and Electronic Media* 33: 159–174; William Hoynes and David Croteau, "Are You on the *Nightline* Guest List?" *Extra!* January/February 1989, pp. 1–15.

42. Doug Grow, "Ads Attacking NSP Nuclear Fuel Storage Plan Didn't Meet Standards," *Minneapolis Star Tribune*, November 29, 1991, p. 3B.

43. United Press International, "Nebraska Radio Station Boycotts k.d. lang Over Meat Campaign," June 26, 1990; United Press International, "Station Owner Bans Country Star's Music," June 28, 1990.

44. Associated Press, "Radio Stations Shy Away from Anti-Hudson Ads" and "Supreme Court Rules Firms Can Prevent Unions from Distributing Leaflets on Company Property," *Minneapolis Star Tribune*, November 30, 1991, p. 2D.

45. Lawrence Soley and Robert Craig, "Advertising Pressures on Newspapers: A Survey," *Journal of Advertising* 21:1–10; Adam Platt, "Angry Dealers Pull TV Ads," *Washington Journalism Review*, September 1991; Lawrence Soley, "'The Power of the Press Has a Price,'" *Extra!* July/August 1997, pp. 11–13.

46. Jack Sissors and Lincoln Bumba, *Advertising Media Planning* (Lincolnwood, Ill.: NTC Business Books, 1990), p. 216.

47. For an example of how this was done to *Ms.* magazine, see Gloria Steinem, "Sex, Lies & Advertising," *Ms.*, July/August 1990, pp. 18–28.

48. Don Imus, quoted in Mark Landler, "Merging Voices that Roar: Is a Radio Deal too Big?" *New York Times*, June 21, 1996, p. C1.

49. Geraldine Fabrikant, "Two Radio Giants to Merge, Forming Biggest U.S. Chain," *New York Times*, June 21, 1996, p. A1, C5.

50. Melanie Wells, "Hicks Muse Tunes in American Music as Next Target," *USA Today*, August 26, 1997, p. 3B.

51. S. Robert Lichter, Stanley Rothman, and Linda Lichter, *The Media Elite* (Bethesda, Md.: Adler & Adler, 1986), p. 30.

52. Jim Gogek, "Talk Radio Catches Static for Cynicism in U.S." *San Diego Union,* January 3, 1994, p. A2.

53. Harvey Zuckman and Martin Gaynes, *Mass Communications Law* (St. Paul: West Publishing, 1977), pp. 315–316.

54. Mike Kaszuba, "Can Malls Tell Protestors to Bag It?" *Minneapolis Star Tribune,* January 29, 1995, p. 1B; Jim Carpenter and Lawrence Soley, "Citizens Must Be Able to Exercise First Amendment Rights in Malls," *Milwaukee Journal Sentinel,* January 30, 1996, p. 9A; Sam Roberts, "Taking Liberty Inside the Mall," *Sacramento Bee,* January 8, 1995, p. F3.

5

Pirate Radio: The Early Rebellion

The term "pirate radio" is often used to describe unlicensed radio stations because the first unlicensed stations that broadcast popular music to the United States and Europe were located aboard ships in international waters. The earliest unlicensed, offshore station appears to have been RKXR, which was based on the S.S. *City of Panama*, a floating gambling casino anchored off the California coast in 1933.

The offshore station took the FRC by surprise; the agency was not sure whether it had jurisdiction over the station because the ship was registered in Panama and anchored in coastal waters. Rather than merely seizing and silencing the station, the U.S. government demanded that Panama rescind the ship's registry, which Panama did. Then in August 1933, the Coast Guard seized the vessel and towed it to Los Angeles, where its gambling equipment was impounded and its transmitter permanently silenced.[1]

Twenty-five years later, unlicensed, ship-based stations appeared off the European coast. The term "pirate stations" was used to describe these offshore operations, and the term has subsequently been applied to all unlicensed stations. The first offshore European station, Radio Mercur, appeared in 1958, broadcasting from a ship named the *Cheeta Mercur* anchored outside territorial waters off the Danish coast. The FM station filled a programming void in Denmark by playing rock music, which was popular among young Danes but was not carried on licensed stations.[2] Unlike free radio stations, Radio Mercur was operated by an entrepreneur, and its purpose was to make a profit through the sale of advertising time.

In 1960 an offshore radio station began broadcasting to Holland, and in 1961 ship-based stations began broadcasting to Belgium and Sweden. The Dutch government quickly silenced a pirate television station, TV-Nordzee, that appeared in 1964, but allowed Radio Veronica, the offshore radio station, to remain on the air for many years. The Belgian station, *Tyll Eulenspiegel*, broadcast only briefly, having foundered in a storm, and Radio Nord was shut down by the Swedish government in 1962.

Offshore broadcasting picked up steam in 1964, when Radio Caroline, Radio Atlantic, Radio London, and Radio 390 started broadcasting to Great Britain from ships in the English Channel. In 1965 Radio Essex appeared, and in 1966 Radio Scotland, Radio England, and Radio 270 dropped their anchors off the British coast. All were commercial, carrying ads for British-based firms, and quite profitable.

The profiteering of these offshore entrepreneurs eventually did them in. The stations began selling advertising time to candidates for public office, even though the British political system provided candidates with equal access to the BBC. As University of Minnesota professor Don Browne, noted:

> In September 1966, however, a Captain Ramsey McLaren used Britain Radio to advertise his candidacy for a seat on the Harwich Town Council; in the same month, the Scottish Nationalist Party announced that it was considering the use of Radio Scotland to aid in the recruiting drive for the Party; in January 1967, the manager of Radio Scotland announced his intention to use his station to support his own candidacy for a seat in the House of Commons; and in May 1967, some Conservative Party candidates purchased air time on . . . Radio 270 in conjunction with local elections being held in Scarborough.[3]

The pirates also threw their support to Conservative party candidates, hoping that a Conservative political victory would lead to their legalization and the birth of commercial broadcasting in Britain.

These actions outraged members of Parliament, particularly Labour members. In June 1967 Parliament passed the Marine, etc. Broadcasting (Offences) Bill, which took effect on August 15. The bill prohibited British citizens from working for the pirate stations, forbade British businesses from advertising on them, and stopped British ships from ferrying supplies to the pirate vessels. At the end of July, Radio England and Radio 390 shut down. On August 14, the day before the bill went into effect, Radio Scotland, Radio 270, and Radio London signed off. Only Radio Caroline remained on the air, bringing in supplies from continental Europe and lining up multinational companies as advertisers. The radio station managed to survive until 1980, when its vessel sank during a storm.

The First Wave

Although these European-based, offshore stations inspired unlicensed broadcasting in the United States, the U.S. pirate stations that went on the air in late 1960s and early 1970s differed from their European counterparts in several ways. First and foremost, the U.S. broadcasters were dedicated to the counterculture of the 1960s, not profits. They were noncommercial and cost their operators money; they didn't make money. Second, the U.S. pirates, unlike the European offshore stations, played a great variety of music, not just Top 40 tunes, thus stretching the boundaries of pop music. Recording artists such as the MC5 and Phil Ochs, who rarely got airplay on commercial stations, were staples of the pirate stations. Third, U.S. pirates tried to serve their local communities, most of which had no local radio outlets. In contrast, the offshore stations tried to reach as large an audience as possible, thereby making themselves more attractive to advertisers. Fourth, the U.S. pirates featured talk shows, call-ins, and political commentary, making them more similar to today's micropower radio stations than the European offshore stations.

One of the earliest U.S. pirate stations was WRAD, which took to the air in the fall of 1969 in Yonkers, New York. The station was operated by Alan H. Weiner, then a teenager, who felt that Yonkers needed a station of its own because every station heard there originated in New York City.

WRAD broadcast on 1620 AM from a modified military surplus transmitter located in the basement of Weiner's parents' home. In a 1996 interview Weiner described what happened: "WRAD was on the air for two weeks before we were ratted on and the FCC came, and my friends and I ran out the back door."[4] The FCC issued Weiner a warning against operating an unlicensed station.

Several months later, Weiner started another station, WKOV, which also broadcast to Yonkers on 1620 AM. The station operated between December 1969 and mid-1971, when the FCC finally shut it down. "My friends and I were getting together and getting more political," said Weiner about their motivations for starting WKOV.

> We decided to get on the air and discuss what was happening politically. And we did. We talked about the war, the government, and everything else that was going on. . . . My friends and I believed that Yonkers needed its own station and didn't have one. To this day, it doesn't. We felt there were no stations on the air that were open to listeners. They were very orchestrated and tightly controlled. It was out of civil disobedience that we went on the air.

WKOV broadcast first with 50 watts and then 300 watts, carrying folk and rock music by Country Joe, Phil Ochs, and other artists who rarely got air time on large New York City stations, which filled the airwaves with the commercial sounds of the Monkees and Three Dog Night. WKOV became the voice of the Yonkers community. "We encouraged our listeners to call in anytime during the broadcasts and if there was anything they really wanted to discuss, we would do it between records," Weiner recalled. "It made for some pretty interesting programming."

In early 1970, one of WKOV's listeners, J. P. Ferraro, started another station, WFSR, which shared the 1620 frequency with WKOV. Weiner's station broadcast on Mondays, Wednesdays, Fridays, and Saturdays, and Ferraro's station broadcast on Tuesdays, Thursdays, and Sundays. In March 1970, as FM started generating more listenership, the Yonkers broadcasters started WXMN-FM, named for

Edwin Armstrong's experimental station, W2XMN, which broadcast briefly during the 1930s. WXMN was joined in March 1970 by WSEX, which also broadcast on 87.9 MHz FM with 250 watts of power. Together, the two AM and two FM stations formed the Falling Star Network, which signed on daily at noon. The network was open about its location and its reasons for operating.

The stations were operated by volunteers. "We had thirty or forty people—mostly kids. People would come in with their own music and play it for three or four hours," Weiner recalled. "At night we'd have 'rap sessions,' as we called them, talking about the war, the government, music and things. It was a real gas. I had more fun then than with any radio venture I've done since."

Community response to the stations was generally favorable, particularly among the parents of teens who worked there. "The reaction of parents was very positive—thinking that we were doing things that were very positive and constructive. The only complaints were from our neighbors . . . [the station] blocked out Channel 7, which carried the 'Brady Bunch,' so we shut down for the time it was on."

One group that was not impressed with the Falling Star Network was a local ham radio group, composed of older white men, who believed the pirate broadcasters to be a bunch of Communists. "They were responsible for shutting us down," claimed Weiner. "The ham radio group kept putting pressure on the FCC to shut us down."

Eventually, the FCC acted. It raided the homes of Weiner and Ferraro, confiscated all of their equipment, and arrested the young radio broadcasters. Weiner described it as "a search and destroy mission." He and Ferraro eventually pleaded no contest to the charges, received probation, and thereafter pulled the plug on their radio stations.

The Falling Star Network stations operated almost without interruption for a year and a half before being shut down by the FCC. The stations demonstrated that the FCC's requirement that licensed broadcasters be well-financed is primarily designed to restrict access to the airwaves, rather than to ensure that listeners get an uninterrupted stream of programming. If a small group of teenagers can keep four radio stations going for over a year and a half, community and labor groups can easily do the same. Since the FCC is well aware that many free radio stations have survived for years—even decades—it is also aware that its policy requiring potential broadcasters to be well-financed is a straw man designed to ensure that only the rich have access to the airwaves.

Several unlicensed radio stations took to the air around the time that the Falling Star Network went off the air. In Bloomington, Indiana, Bruce Quinn, a legally blind radio buff, was derailed by the FCC in his efforts to obtain a license permitting him to work at aboveground stations. Rather than issuing him a license, the FCC granted him a "blind endorsement," restricting the duties he could perform at a station. "They felt my blindness would hamper my ability to work," reported Quinn. "I was bitter about that."

In response to the FCC's discrimination, Quinn started Jolly Roger Radio, which broadcast on AM and FM from a studio in his living room. The station targeted college students at Indiana University with rock, folk, and country music interspersed with commentary. Quinn served as Jolly Roger Radio's program director, and volunteers, many of whom were Indiana University students, served as engineers and disc jockeys. Station personnel donned *nommes de guerre,* such as "the Flying Dutchman" and "Joan of Arc." Joan, for example, was a folklore student who aired Iranian santir music, Irish folk tunes, and other music related to her field of study.

Unlike the Falling Star Network stations, Jolly Roger Radio remained on the air for over a decade, largely because of its limited hours of operation and distance from a FCC field office. However, in November 1980 the FCC finally raided the station, arresting Quinn and two volunteers. Each were fined $250 and given probation.

After his probation ended, Quinn temporarily revived the station in January 1983, but shut it down several months later, after the FCC concluded that blind endorsements were discriminatory. Because of the FCC policy reversal, Quinn decided to apply again for an operator's license.[5]

Another unlicensed station, using the call letters WTFC, appeared on Christmas Eve 1964, broadcasting holiday music to New Castle County, Delaware. Unlike the Falling Star Network stations and Jolly Roger Radio, WTFC operated intermittently, rather than continuously, and survived for twenty-four years. During that time, it broadcast on 640 KHz AM from just two locations: a room above a garage and a shack in the operator's backyard.

WTFC initially broadcast on holidays and weekends but occasionally had a daily schedule during its decades of operation. Its announcer referred to himself as "Carl Stromberg," a name taken from the now-defunct brand of Stromberg Carlsen radio receivers, and he played a mix of popular tunes.

The station was started when Stromberg and a neighbor were teenagers. "The magic of radio attracted us," Stromberg said. In later years, Stromberg continued to operate the station because it was "a lot of fun . . . allowing a lot of people who would never have gotten on radio to get on the air. Some would have a [political or social] agenda and get on and say whatever the hell they wanted."[6]

Although the FCC searched for the station for nearly two decades, the agency failed to locate it. WTFC went off the air in 1988, after its transmitter tower collapsed.[7] The station demonstrated that, with a little inventiveness and persistence, unlicensed radio broadcasters can avoid being muzzled by the FCC.

The Second Wave

WTFC, Jolly Roger Radio, and the Falling Star stations were not the only unlicensed stations broadcasting in the United States during the late 1960s and early 1970s. There were others, including Voice of the Purple Pumpkin, Radio

Clandestine, and WGHP. But it was in the mid-1970s and early 1980s that a new wave of free radio stations appeared, openly challenging the FCC's rules against unlicensed broadcasting. These stations took to the air in response to the corporate-developed, album-oriented rock format on FM, which proved to be as suffocating as the Top 40 format had been during the '60s. The format dictated what could be discussed over the air, imposed stifling playlists on disc jockeys, and deprived radio of its local voice, replacing it with a canned approach that made all album-oriented rock stations—regardless of the city they were in—sound the same.

Teenagers John Calabro and Perry Cavalieri, residents of a Brooklyn housing project, challenged this corporate control in November 1975 by starting WCPR, which they hoped would resuscitate rock radio.[8] "We were always music fans," explained Calabro, "but some time in the mid-1970s we stopped being thrilled with radio. It was boring—but not as boring as now."[9] They began by broadcasting Beatles music using a homemade, low-power FM transmitter that covered a five block area, but then they acquired an AM transmitter from another unlicensed radio broadcaster, Gary Stevens, who operated WGOR—gorilla radio. "It was a 1943 Collins transmitter. It was big and heavy—over 100 pounds," recalled Calabro. With this transmitter, the teenagers were able to blanket Brooklyn and outlying areas with music and talk, generated by callers.

"There was no local programming," said Calabro about commercial radio in those days.

> Radio had become so huge. It was a multimillion dollar business, and Brooklyn, which is bigger than most cities, had no local programming. The number one reason we went on the air was there was no open phone-in radio shows . . . there was no local call-in show. There were national talk shows—we could tune into Larry King on sixteen separate places on the dial—but there were no local talk shows.

WCPR and other stations operated by Calabro and Cavalieri over the years invited listeners to call in and discuss whatever they wanted. Their philosophy was to "open the phone lines and let people say whatever was on their mind." WCPR did this by using *phone loops,* which kept the FCC from tracing where calls originated and ended. Phone loops were telephone numbers used by the phone company for testing lines. The phone company would assign an unused number, such as 667-6667, to one part of the loop and another number, such as 667-6661, to the other, and two different phone lines could be connected by calling these numbers. The radio broadcasters would call one of the loop numbers, announce the other over the air, and when a listener called, a connection was established. The phone conversation was then broadcast over the air.

"We discovered loops years earlier totally by accident," Calabro reported. "A friend of ours was a phone freak—into all these zany things about phones. He gave us five numbers. It sounded like fun. You call the number, hear a steady tone, and when it goes away, you're on the phone with a total stranger. We realized this must be some kind of telco [telephone company] system." Calabro and Cavalieri later decided that they could use this system to operate call-in radio shows with untraceable numbers.

One of the down sides of using loops is that one caller can tie up the system by not hanging up. When this occurred during a WCPR broadcast in January 1976, Calabro and Cavalieri broadcast their real phone number over the air in order to open the station to listeners. FCC monitors recorded and traced the number, and WCPR was busted on February 7, 1976. Because Calabro and Cavalieri were not yet twenty-one years old, they got away with a warning. After that, they laid low . . . for a while.

On New Year's Eve 1977, Calabro and Cavalieri returned to the air with WFAT, a 50-watt AM station operating on 1620 KHz and featuring popular music and call-ins. The station opened with the announcement, "At the tone, the time will be 11:30. This is WFAT in New York," followed by a Beatles tune.

The station was located in Perry Cavalieri's apartment bedroom on the eighth floor of the Marborough public housing project in Brooklyn. The same old Collins transmitter they had used for WCPR energized WFAT, and its antenna consisted of a 125-foot wire running from Perry's bedroom across the courtyard to the building next door.

Like WCPR, the station featured music and an open mike, allowing listeners to call in and say what was on their mind, and employed telephone loops to keep the FCC from locating and silencing the station. Because of its accessibility to listeners, WFAT called itself "New York's only locally-originated AM late-night open-topic phone-in talk show." The station cultivated a following, including a group of regular callers, from as far away as New England and West Virginia, where the station's AM signal bounced at night. Calabro described the format: "The music would stop for two hours to take phone calls—it was totally free—it was free radio. . . . We weren't political, but if someone wanted to talk about politics, they were free to. We made our statement by existing."

The station's sporadic operation and the large number of apartments near Cavalieri's made it difficult for the FCC to locate and silence the station. To locate WFAT, the FCC formed a task force that staked out several locations, including Cavalieri's project.

The station operated for sixteen months before Cavalieri and Calabro spotted FCC agents carrying tracking equipment in the project courtyard around two o'clock in the morning on April 19, 1979. WFAT announced: "This is it. WFAT has to leave the air." Before signing off, Howie, a regular caller to the station, dialed in and yelled, "Rock n' Roll forever!" The station then went off the air, and Calabro and Cavalieri started disassembling their equipment, including cutting the wire that served as their antenna. Because the elevator in the building was not working, the FCC agents had to walk up the stairs to the apartment, giving the broadcasters additional time to take apart and hide their equipment. The federal agents knocked at the door and when Perry answered, one said, "You have a very nice sounding radio station."[10]

The FCC's silencing of WFAT was part of a larger federal campaign to silence unlicensed stations in the New York area. Between WFAT's sign-on and its silencing, nearly two dozen other free stations were on the air, including WGOR, WPNJ (named for operators Paul, Nick, and Joe), and WISY-FM, which originated on Staten Island. One by one, the FCC silenced them, even though the stations did not interfere with licensed, corporate-owned stations.

Pirate stations appeared in other cities during this period. In Los Angeles, Richard Dorwart, crippled by osteogenesis imperfecta, a congenital illness, went on the air with KDOR-AM, which provided an alternative to LA's commercial radio scene. In New England, several pirate stations broadcast, and in Lanesville, New York, a low-power pirate TV station operated until it was shut down by the FCC in 1977.[11] Numerous pirate stations, like the Voice of Voyager, took to the shortwave band as well, but since these were targeted to shortwave listeners rather than local communities, they had little influence on the development of free radio.[12]

The New Wave

The FCC's repression did not retard the growth of unlicensed broadcasting; on the contrary, many stations challenged the FCC's authority during the early 1980s, when commercial rock stations refused to air music by iconoclastic new wave bands like the Runaways, the Dead Kennedys, and the Clash. When new wave groups did get airtime, it was on noncommercial college stations and unlicensed radio stations, such as Jamestown, New York's WDOG-AM, and Milwaukee's WTPS ("The Pirate Station").

During the mid-1980s, WDOG operated every other weekend on 1620 KHz, one of the frequencies most popular with unlicensed AM broadcasters. WDOG's slogan was, "Broadcasting to no one in particular," and its chief disc jockey was T. E. Magnatron, who aired punk rock, technopop, and reggae music.[13]

Milwaukee's WTPS took to the air in early 1983, broadcasting on 104.5 MHz FM to the northeastern part of the city, not far from the University of Wisconsin at Milwaukee campus. The station soon garnered a following, and a *Milwaukee Journal* poll found it to be the sixth most-listened-to station in the city, despite its small coverage area.[14] During this time, WTPS was audible within only a one-mile radius of the transmitter's location. It has since changed its transmitter location, power of operation, and frequency several times, in response to federal busts, station interference, and snoopy reporters.

From its inception, WTPS aired new music from groups such as Human Sexual Response, the Dead Boys and the The. Its raison d'etre was that commercial radio stations and even college stations in Milwaukee refused to carry the new music format.

"We put the station on as a protest," explained Bill Stevens, the on-air name of the station's founder. Stevens had been the program director at college radio station WMSE, which aired punk rock and new wave music during 1981 and 1982, but was fired when the school's administrators decided to change the station's format. "You could say we did a little housekeeping," the college's vice president arrogantly told *Milwaukee* magazine about the firing. "I will not beat around the bush about saying that [our college] is a conservative engineering school, and that is the kind of image we want to present. We simply do not have in mind being known as a punk rock and new wave school."[15]

After being fired, Stevens and several disc jockeys, who had also been fired from WMSE, started WTPS, using pseudonyms like Commander Todd, Big Daddy, and Mort the Hump. Over the years, over two dozen other people have served as disc jockeys on WTPS.

The station was on the air for less than a year when it was busted by the FCC, which learned about the station from a newspaper article, sent to the commission anonymously. "I believe it was people from WMSE who turned us in," said Stevens, who eventually paid a $300 fine for operating the station.

WTPS then moved to cable for a year, but resurfaced on 107.1 FM in 1985, broadcasting from Milwaukee's Eastside, the city's chic and trendy neighborhood. There the station played hide-and-seek with the FCC for years. It was forced to move up to 107.3 in 1992 when a new commercial station in a nearby city interfered with its signal. In 1992 the station moved to Milwaukee's Southside, a working class neighborhood, where it established itself as "Milwaukee's Community Radio," airing announcements for a variety of community groups, including Volunteers of Greater Milwaukee, the Milwaukee Youth Theater Group, and the Boulevard Theater Ensemble. The announcements were produced by volunteer disc jockeys using on-air names such as Michelle, J. W Towcar, and Harry Lippermore. As Stevens described it, "We're more than a jukebox. . . . We want to provide a community focus for community issues. Radio is most successful when it's local."

In mid-1996, WTPS moved to 99.9 FM after an engineering study showed that a signal on that frequency would not interfere with any station. "We conducted two engineering studies," Stevens explained. "One was to find out if we could put a noncommercial station on the air and the other to find if there was any room anywhere else on the dial—and they came up with 99.9 to comply with the [noninterference] rules." The engineering study showed that there were no other frequencies left in Milwaukee for putting on new stations—broadcasting corporations had already gobbled up every available frequency.

WTPS promotes itself and informs listeners of its frequency changes by distributing a new music "play list" at record stores, other gathering places, and on the Worldwide Web. The station even airs remote broadcasts from public parks on holidays, such as the Fourth of July. For several years, the station was played in local record stores and bars. However, most people learn about the station by word of mouth. Once someone learns about the station, they can program their radios to it because WTPS is on twenty-four hours a day, 365 days a year.

The success of WTPS inspired another station, which broadcast from the Milwaukee suburb of West Bend. Calling itself Z-97 and broadcasting with 10 watts of power, the station aired new music from the home of Don Anderson, who operated the station using the on-air name Matt Kincayde. Commercial stations operating near 97 MHz quickly complained to the FCC, which busted Anderson, issuing a "notice of apparent liability" and a fine of $1,000. Anderson responded to the FCC action by shutting down his station, but warned, "I think you'll see more and more pirates, because people want to hear that type of music."[16]

Anderson was right. People did want to hear this music, and many listeners tuned to unlicensed stations to hear it. WKEY-FM, an unlicensed station broadcasting from the Cleveland suburb of South Euclid with just 40 watts of power, was on the air for only a few months in late 1988 and early 1989, but managed nevertheless to attract enough listeners to be listed by the Arbitron rating service. Although the FCC conceded that the station did not interfere with any licensed stations, the agency nevertheless shut WKEY down in April 1989, presumably because it took listeners away from commercial stations and their advertisers.[17]

Other unlicensed stations, including WGNK (aka Radio Free New England), Daytona Beach's Radio X (103.5 FM), and Tampa's 87X (also known as Radio Free Ybor and Radio Free Tampa), also played new music. Of these, only 87X operated as a neighborhood radio station, speaking for local residents rather than just the individual or group operating the station.

Radio Free Ybor was started by Chuck Stephens and Billy Budget, residents of Ybor City, a recently gentrified section of Tampa known for its boutiques, nightlife, and restaurants on 7th Avenue, and its poverty off the avenue. Stephens, who had made headlines in the *Tampa Tribune* because he made a living putting change in parking meters for 7th Avenue entrepreneurs, suggested to Billy Budget, a local handyman, activist, and punk rocker, that they start an FM station, an idea that excited Budget. Stephens combed surplus stores for a transmitter while Budget combed catalogs and classified ads in electronics magazines. Budget eventually purchased a mail-order Panaxis transmitter, amplifier, and antenna, which transmitted at 87.9 MHz with 30 watts of power.[18]

The station kicked off with a broadcast from an Ybor City backyard in February 1995, with Stephens spinning punk rock albums and some members of a local band, Magadog, also taking turns as disc jockeys. The first listeners to the station were patrons and employees of Ybor Pizza and Subs, a local hangout that tuned its radio to 87.9 FM.

The station also did a few broadcasts from the Blue Chair Music Store, an independent record store in a huge building on 7th Avenue, which hosted parties and concerts by local punk bands. When events were taking place at the Blue Chair, Budget would set up the transmitter and do live broadcasts from there. Eventually, 87X was sponsoring parties at the Blue Chair.

One of the disc jockeys for these parties was Kelly Kombat, who later assumed responsibilities for operating the station. At Kombat's suggestion, 87X instituted a policy of not playing music that denigrated women, races, or ethnic groups, a policy that most corporate-owned stations have yet to adopt.

In June, a local theatrical group, the Hillsborough Moving Company, moved from its office at the Blue Chair, and 87X moved into this space. From then on, the station was on the air twenty-four hours a day, playing new music and covering local events, poetry readings, and concerts.

Unlike traditional pirate stations, Radio Free Ybor was a community effort, whose volunteers included long-time residents, squatters, punks, and even employees of Ybor Pizza and Subs. The volunteer announcers took names such as Miss Chronic, Scott Megatron, and Mister Black. To provide programming to Ybor City's diverse population, the station started playing a variety of music, including punk, ska, reggae, and hip hop, and it served as a community bulletin board, broadcasting announcements for local groups.

Five months after 87X went on the air full time, FCC agents visited the Blue Chair. The agents arrived in the morning when Blue Chair employees, who had partied the night before, were still sleeping at home. So, in the great tradition of the FBI during the Red Scare of the 1950s, the agents visited the elderly owner of the shop next door, Adams City Hatters, flashing their credentials and asking him about the FM antenna on the roof next door. The shop owner knew nothing about the station, but he did inform Blue Chair employees about the visit soon after the store opened.

As a result of the visit, 87X signed off temporarily, but resumed broadcasting in January, when Kombat moved the transmitter to his home. On February 1, 1996, FCC field agents, unbeknownst to Kombat, monitored the broadcasts of 87X from near his home. Three weeks later, the agents again monitored the station, but this time approached Kombat's residence, knocking on the door and demanding to inspect the transmitter. The disc jockey at the station told them that they couldn't come in, so they left. The agents returned to the apartment again on February 26, monitored the broadcasts, and later sent Kombat their usual letter, threatening him with a $10,000 fine and one year in prison.

As a result of the threats, Kombat moved the transmitter to an office outside Ybor City, from which the station broadcast for a couple of months. After the office's owner became worried that the FCC would locate and bust the station, Kombat again moved the transmitter, first to an apartment, then to a house, and then to a location in Tampa's Seminole Heights, an area with a high concentration of artists, from where it broadcast as Radio Free Tampa. "We changed the name of the station to indicate our loftier ambitions," said Kombat about the name change.[19]

During 1997, 87X increased its power with a new 40-watt transmitter and had a dozen volunteers, who used on-air names such as Jessica, Kathy, Milk Dud, and Jakira Chaos. All developed their shows without interference from Kombat, who oversaw the station's day-to-day operations, such as making out the schedule and making sure that volunteers showed up at their scheduled times. For example, Jessica had a show that interspersed music with political discussions and interviews. Her guests included members of Uhuru, an African-American empowerment group involved in the 1996 protests against St. Petersburg police brutality, representatives of the state Greens party, and other local activists. The station was so successful that it was named "best radio station" by Tampa's alternative weekly, the *Weekly Planet*, which described the station as "a refreshing breeze in the simmering desert."[20]

87X wasn't the only unlicensed station broadcasting to the Tampa-St. Petersburg area during 1996 and 1997. There were others, including the Party Pirate, Lutz Community Radio and the West Tampa Delight, an African-American station. Despite their different ideologies and different formats, the stations' operators were in contact with each other, forming a loosely organized group of unlicensed broadcasters.

The Party Pirate (102.1 MHz) was started by Doug Brewer, who is licensed by the FCC to repair transmitting equipment. It started as a low-power holiday station in 1991, broadcasting Christmas music to Temple Terrace, a suburb northwest of Tampa. After operating on holidays for several years, the station slowly increased its broadcast times and power.

By 1996 the station was on weekdays from 5:00 p.m. to midnight and twenty-four hours a day on weekends with 65 watts of power. The station's first announcers were Brewer and a few friends, who primarily played rock music but also took listener call-ins and willingly interrupted the music schedule to accommodate callers.

In mid-1996, the station attempted to broaden its base by recruiting announcers and disc jockeys using on-air announcements and leaflets, which read:

> Do you have programming ideas, or a desire to have a program slot on the air? Perhaps you would like to do a music program or a community awareness program. Do you know of a church or civic organization that would like to have access to the airwaves? The opportunity is here NOW, but we need you to ACT NOW. There is no charge to any person to gain access to this valuable community service.[21]

As a result of the recruitment effort, The Party Pirate attracted over a dozen volunteer disc jockeys and announcers and adopted the name Temple Terrace Community Radio.

The station continued to play mostly rock music, but disc jockeys were free to play and say whatever they pleased. Eric Ericson, the on-air name for a volunteer disc jockey who had worked in commercial broadcasting for ten years, played heavy metal; disk jockeys Gabi and Jen played modern rock; and Paul "The New Music Guy" played new wave, reggae, and technopop. Each put in a few hours every week at the station.

In an interview, Eric Ericson said that he volunteered because working at a corporate-owned station is an atrophy-inducing experience. The television station where Ericson was employed had been recently bought by a large corporation. "A big corporation bought us and now we have big brother staring down our throats," Ericson commented.

He compared his work at 102.1 with working at commercial stations: "Working here is fun," but "most of the deejays at the local [commercial] stations are puppets with program directors telling them what to play, advertising managers telling them what to pitch, and general managers telling them what to say."[22]

Another volunteer commented, "No where else in the Bay area can you hear this much variety on the radio. Each DJ is his or her own program director. No more 'if you talk about that, you're fired.'"[23] In fact, the station never restricted what could be said on the air, producing a steady stream of sexual chitchat and controversial comments from deejays and listeners.[24]

Lutz Community Radio, which was on-the-air twenty-four hours a day in a small town just north of Tampa, was operated by Lonnie Kobres, a soft-spoken man whom Tampa broadcasting stations describe as a "right-wing extremist" because he is part of the "constitutionalist movement" or "freedom movement." The 96.7 FM station, based in Kobres's home, was "dedicated to the defense of God, Family, and Country" through programs on survival, organic gardening, herbal medicine, and home schooling. "There is an artificial society that's been created and we've been dumbed down, so to speak, on how to be self-sufficient," Kobres explained in an interview. Lutz Community Radio was designed to counter this process and make listeners less dependent on government, corporations, and other institutions of the "New World Order."[25]

The station primarily broadcast programs that originated on the USA Patriot and Eagle Radio satellite networks, but it also produced a small amount of local programming—until it was first raided by the FCC on March 7, 1996, and its production equipment was confiscated. Its programs addressed people who "are tired of being played for fools by an elitist-dominated media that refuses to provide information needed to cast a meaningful vote," said Kobres, who put the station back on the air shortly after the FCC bust.[26]

The programming was highly critical of the federal government and the New World Order but had rules that could not be broken. Advocating the overthrow of the government, anti-Semitism, and racism were prohibited. "We don't advocate the overthrow of the government," said Kobres. "It's already been overthrown.

That's what we're against." As for anti-Semitism and racism, Kobres described them as divide-and-conquer tactics that pit opponents of the New World Order against each other.

Kobres selected 96.7 MHz because no other station in the area operated on that frequency. Kobres pointed out that because Lutz Community Radio operated with under 50 watts of power, it was not interfering with any other station. Despite this, the FCC, backed with a phalanx of federal marshals, raided Kobres's home again on November 19, 1997, and seized his transmitter.[27] Kobres provided his explanation for the bust: "They raided my station because they're fearful of the words of truth. The first amendment is one of their greatest obstacles. . . . If we played 90 percent music and 10 percent talk like other stations, we wouldn't have been raided."

The West Tampa Delight is the station of "Blackbeard," who broadcasts intermittently, always beginning at 6:00 p.m. on 98.3 MHz, the frequency used several years earlier by another unlicensed African-American station called Base FM.[28] "This is something I really want to do because Tampa is the only major city that doesn't have a Black FM station," explained Blackbeard, who plays reggae, rhythm & blues, and hip hop, frequently recorded by local musicians. "We want everyone to know about the vast amount of talent Tampa has to offer." [29] But unlike 87X, where Blackbeard formerly worked as a deejay, the West Tampa Delight airs songs that demean women, an issue over which Blackbeard and 87X's Kelly Kombat differ. "I play what's popular," said Blackbeard about Kombat's criticism of his programming.

Blackbeard uses a transmitter and other equipment borrowed from Doug Brewer and spins his own records and those given him by local bands and promoters. The station also features "shout outs" and "what's happenings," keeping listeners informed about events in Tampa's African-American neighborhoods.

The West Tampa Delight has a format similar to Zoom Black Magic Radio, which has broadcast to Fresno, California's African-American population since 1985. Like Tampa and other cities, Fresno does not have an FM—or even an AM—black-oriented station. As Walter Dunn, Jr., the founder of Zoom Black Magic Radio, put it: "There's a black community of 100,000 people in the San Joaquin Valley, and there isn't a radio station around with a black personality on the air. We're filling a need."[30]

Dunn calls himself the "Black Rose of Fresno" on the air, where he is joined by "Daddy Rich," "Iceberg," "Mellow Yellow," and other announcers, who play jazz, blues, gospel, and hip hop peppered with community announcements, news analysis, and challenging patter. "Welcome to slave quarters radio," the Black Rose announces from a trailer behind his home, which functions as the station's studio.

Like Lutz Community Radio, Zoom Black Magic Radio's transmitter was seized by the FCC, which also slapped him with a $2,000 fine in 1987. Despite these actions, the Black Rose returned to the air within weeks from his trailer studio, which he hooked to his car and towed to a nearby shopping center, from where he broadcast defiantly. "I let them know they aren't going to intimidate me. Let them get me if that's what they want," Dunn said about the FCC. The broadcast from the shopping center lasted less than an hour before police asked him to leave; Dunn's presence was creating traffic congestion as motorists slowed down to wave at him.[31]

In 1989 the FCC again raided Zoom Black Magic Radio and seized its transmitter. Dunn believed that this raid took place because he refused to pay the fine levied two years earlier. Shortly after this seizure, Dunn vowed to return to the air. "I'm going to get another transmitter and fire it up. It will take a couple of weeks or so, but the black community is going to have a black radio station," Dunn said. True to his word, Dunn returned to the air, challenging the FCC and declaring that the agency's actions violated his constitutional right to free speech.[32]

The Tidal Wave

Punk rockers, disenfranchised African-Americans, '60s activists, and opponents of the New World Order are not the only people who operate or listen to unlicensed stations. Fans of oldies, blues, folk, and even classical music have discovered that since they are nonprofit, pirate stations provide better programming than commercial, licensed stations. Commercial stations produce programming in which advertised products can be sold; they don't exist to entertain, inform, or educate listeners.

Pirate station operators, by contrast, are dedicated to their music and listeners; profit is not part of the equation. Because of this dedication, many pirate stations have attracted substantial followings. In New York City, pirate station WHOT was on the air for much of the 1980s, airing oldies and classic rock on AM and FM. WHOT personalities like "Jim Nasium" were so popular that they were recruited as disc jockeys for Radio Newyork International, a short-lived offshore station that broadcast off the coast of New York in 1987 and 1988. WHOT was eventually silenced by the FCC in July 1989.[33]

Another pirate disc jockey known for his political commentary and music selections was "Pirate Joe," whose station, KSUN, went on the air in New York City between 1980 and 1982 at ten o'clock after WNYE, the station of the New York Board of Education, shut down for the night. Pirate Joe took calls, held discussions of events in El Salvador and Nicaragua, and spun recordings rarely heard on commercial stations. In 1983 Pirate Joe moved to a pirate station with more broadcasting power, KPRC, which broadcast on AM, FM, and shortwave to much of the Northeastern United States. The station was eventually tracked down and silenced by the FCC. After that, Pirate Joe resurfaced on Radio Newyork International.[34]

The popularity of WHOT and KSUN and the blandness of New York commercial stations led to a tidal wave of pirate stations during the early to mid-1980s. During 1982–1983, the New York City area had approximately twenty pirate stations, including Rebel Music Radio, which aired anti-war programming and music such as Bob Dylan's "Masters of War" on 1616 KHz; WBUZ-FM, whose operator was busted twice by the FCC; WJPL, whose announcer was "Johnny Lightening," a Brooklyn-born railroad worker; and the Crystal Goblin, whose station, WART, cultivated a substantial audience on 1620 KHz AM. In New England, there were dozens of other pirate stations on the air—enough to form the Free Radio Campaign, which had 100 affiliates and even more supporters. The campaign demanded a change in FCC licensing policy, something the FCC completely ignored.[35]

The FCC ignored complaints about its licensing policies, leading to a further growth of pirate broadcasting during the mid-1980s, including several shortwave political pirates, such as Tangerine Radio, operated by an anarchist collective; WYMN ("Women's Radio"), a feminist station operated by pirates Cindy and Jenny; and Radio KNBS ("Radio Cannabis"), which advocated the legalization of marijuana. The mid-1980s was also when the first U.S. micropower stations appeared, broadcasting on FM as part of larger political movements.

NOTES

1. Tom Kneitel, "The World's First High Seas Pirate Broadcaster," *Popular Communication*, August 1983, pp. 10–12.

2. Walter B. Emery, *National and International Systems of Broadcasting* (East Lansing, Mich.: Michigan State University Press, 1969), pp. 560–595.

3. Don R. Browne, "The BBC and the Pirates: A Phase in the Life of a Prolonged Monopoly," *Journalism Quarterly* 1971: 48, 96.

4. Alan Weiner, telephone interview by author, November 22, 1996. Unless otherwise identified, all subsequent remarks by Alan Weiner are from this interview.

5. "Regional News–Indianapolis," United Press International, December 24, 1984, BC cycle; Timothy Aeppel, "'Pirate' Radio Operators Plunder the Airwaves," *Christian Science Monitor*, March 15, 1983, p. 5.

6. Carl Stromberg, telephone interview by author, December 11, 1996.

7. Edward Teach, "Pirates Den," *Popular Communications*, January 1989, pp. 52–53; Dale Dalabrida, "Radio Pirate Sails Local Airwaves for 23 Years," *Fine Times*, August 13, 1987, p. 5.

8. Calabro and Cavalieri were also involved in the aborted Radio Newyork International adventure in 1987.

9. John Calabro, telephone interview by author, December 4, 1996. Unless otherwise identified, all subsequent remarks by John Calabro are from this interview.

10. Francis X. Cline, "About New York: A Sound of Silence on WFAT, Pirate Radio," *New York Times*, April 21, 1979, p. 27.

11. "Pirate Joe and the Kilocycle Kops," *Economist*, April 24, 1982, p. 57.

12. These shortwave stations are discussed in Andrew Yoder, *Pirate Radio* (Solana Beach, Calif.: HighText Publications, 1996). An earlier version of this work was entitled *Pirate Radio Stations* (Commack, N.Y.: CRB Research, 1990). According to John Calabro and other ex-broadcasters, Yoder did not interview them, and the works therefore contain some factual errors.

13. Edward Teach, "Pirates Den: Focus on Free Radio Broadcasting," *Popular Communication,* December 1987, p. 32.

14. Divina Infusino, "721 respondents Show Variety of Tastes in Poll," *Milwaukee Journal,* February 17, 1984.

15. Frank Kuznik, "R.I.P. WMSE," *Milwaukee,* October 1982, p. 92; Bill Stevens, interview by author, March 12, 1997. Unless otherwise identified, all subsequent remarks by Bill Stevens are from this interview.

16. Michael Zahn, "Radio Zahn: Tuning in to FM Programming," *Milwaukee Journal,* May 21, 1991.

17. "Ohio: South Euclid," United Press International, April 7, 1989, BC cycle.

18. Tom Roe, "Left of the Dial," *Weekly Planet,* March 14–20, 1996, pp. 13–17.

19. Kelly Kombat, interview by author, July 18, 1996.

20. "Best Radio Station," *Weekly Planet,* September 26–October 2, 1996, p. 38.

21. "102.1 FM, Temple Terrace Community Radio—About YOUR Radio Station," recruitment leaflet, undated.

22. Eric Ericson, in person interview by author, December 21, 1996.

23. "Radio Ga Ga," *Weekly Planet,* December 19–25, 1996, p. 10.

24. Bruce Orwall, "Mr. Brewer the Pirate Doesn't Rule the Waves, He Just Makes Them," *Wall Street Journal,* October 21, 1997, p. A1.

25. Lonnie Kobres, interview by author, December 23, 1996. Unless otherwise identified, all subsequent remarks by Lonnie Kobres are from this interview.

26. Lee Harris, "Political Pirates Proliferating," *Radio World,* April 17, 1996, p. 6.

27. David Sommer, "Lutz Radio Station Equipment Seized," *Tampa Tribune,* March 9, 1996, p. 1.

28. Terry Krueger, *Florida Low Power Radio Stations* (Tampa, Fla.: Tocobaga Publications, 1996), p. 11. A station of the same name operating on 106.3 MHz was recently busted in Orlando by the FCC. Like the Tampa station, Orlando's The Base 106 carried "street-wise, dance-oriented urban music that teens especially seemed to be discovering," according to Catherine Hinman, "105.1 Gives Nod to Cuts by Familiar Artists," *Orlando Sentinel,* December 13, 1996, p. 40. Also see "Pirate Stations Beware: FCC Shuts Down Pirate Station in Orlando, Florida," press release of FCC's Compliance and Information Bureau, Tampa Field Office, December 11, 1996.

29. Judy Candis, "Underground D.J. Moves to FM," *Tampa Sentinel,* June 25, 1996, p. 12; Blackbeard, interview by author, July 18, 1996.

30. Jim Hougan, "The Covert Spectrum," *Whole Earth Review,* September 22, 1990, p. 105.

31. "The Black Rose Ready to Blossom But May be Nipped in the Bud," United Press International, March 18, 1987, BC cycle.

32. "Black Rose Vows to Return to the Air," United Press International, August 15, 1989, BC cycle.

33. Jim Nasium was actually Perry Cavalieri. See Paul Colford, "Feds Seize Radio Pirates' Gear," *Newsday,* December 13, 1989, p. B3.

34. "Pirate Joe and the Kilocycle Kops," *Economist,* April 24, 1982, p. 57.

35. Ibid.; Colford, "Feds Seize Radio Pirates' Gear"; Timothy Aeppel, "'Pirate' Radio Operators Plunder the Airwaves," *Christian Science Monitor,* March 15, 1983, p. 5; James Barron, "Illegal Radio Operators Transmitting Regularly," *New York Times,* April 24, 1982, p. B26.

6

Microradio:
The Revolution Begins

When police beat Dewayne Readus during a 1983 scuffle at the John Hay Homes housing project in Springfield, Illinois, they were no more aware that their actions would lead to a large-scale revolt than were the Los Angeles cops who beat Rodney King. Unlike the revolt in Los Angeles, the one that started in Springfield was nonviolent, invisible, and international. It triggered the microradio revolt—putting on the air unlicensed, low-power stations that originate in and broadcast to local neighborhoods. The revolt has since spread to other cities and countries.

Unlike the "information revolution" being marketed by Microsoft, IBM, and other corporations, the microradio revolt is low-cost, low-tech, and available to all, regardless of wealth and education. Participants in the microradio revolt do not need to buy computers, software, and modems, they do not need to pay access fees to America Online or to be educated in DOS, Windows, and HTML. They do not even need electricity in their homes. All they need is a $10 transistor radio to receive the messages and a $200 transmitter to send them.

The Roots of the Revolt

Dewayne Readus grew up in the John Hay Homes public housing project, a 600-unit complex of low-rise apartments for low-income families a short distance from President Abraham Lincoln's historic home in Springfield, Illinois. In the 1980s the project was home to approximately 3,000 people, the vast majority of whom were African-American. As in other low-income areas, Hay Homes residents were neglected by local officials, state government, and Springfield's mass media, which were—and continue to be—owned by a few corporations, including Saga Communications Corporation of Michigan, Guy Gannett Communications of Maine, and Neuhoff Broadcasting Corporation, which operates two country music stations in the city. No commercial broadcasting stations are directed to Springfield's 15,000 African-Americans, most of whom live within a one-and-a-half mile radius of the Hay Homes project. The city's only daily newspaper is owned by another distant corporation, Copley Press of California.

Despite the neglect, Hay Homes yards were filled with vegetable gardens, game-playing children, small groups of underemployed or unemployed young men who played with liquor and drugs, and cops, who patrolled the projects and talked to residents like guards to prisoners. In 1983 Readus, partially blinded by glaucoma as a child, was like many young African-American men—unable to find a full-time or even a part-time job. To earn money, he became a disc jockey at project parties, spinning R & B disks and getting drunk. One of these parties turned into a brawl and the police were called. The cops arrived swinging and beat Readus so badly he was completely blinded. After that, he became depressed and drank heavily.[1]

After shaking his depression, Readus became interested in social activism and police accountability rather than parties and alcohol. In 1985 he helped organize the Tenants Rights Association (TRA), which demanded that Hay Homes author-ities be accountable to project residents, rather than the other way around.

To improve TRA's outreach, Mike Townsend, a family friend and professor at Sangamon State University, suggested that Readus start a neighborhood newspa-per. Readus, who has since changed his name to Mbanna Kantako (or "resisting warrior"), replied, "I'm blind, let's do radio. I don't get off on print that much." "My jaw dropped at Mbanna's suggestion," said Townsend, who at the time didn't understand the impact that radio could have on community organizing.[2]

In addition to Kantako's blindness, there are other reasons why the TRA needed to use radio. Kantako explained: "Studies show that 40 percent of black men are illiterate. Newspapers can't get them any information. . . . Besides, given technology today, using print is like using the pony express instead of air freight delivery."[3]

At the next meeting of the TRA, members discussed "the most effective way of getting our message to the people. . . . We discussed starting a newspaper, but we recognized that a large percentage of our people can't read. And a whole lot of them that can read, don't or can't comprehend what they're reading."[4] The group also discussed the legality of operating an FM station without a license from the FCC. However, FCC policies make it illegal not only to operate an FM station without a license, but even to buy a fully-assembled FM transmitter.

As Townsend pointed out, U.S. laws on purchasing an AM or FM transmitter are very restrictive: "I don't know if people know that it's illegal here in the United States to order the little equipment that you have to run a radio station with it as-sembled—it has to be sent to you in pieces so that you have to find some kind of electrical wiz that can put it together for you, but the same company, here in the United States, can sell the same transmitter completely put together in any other country, but not to our own people in this country."[5] Napoleon Williams, who operates an unlicensed FM station in nearby Decatur, puts it more succinctly: "It's amazing. You can buy an Uzi fully assembled, but it's illegal to buy one of these [transmitters] fully assembled."[6]

The group weighed the legality of operating a transmitter, and concluded that the benefits far outweighed the risks. "We're not even concerned about the FCC regulations. Clearly they were designed before blacks were allowed to hold their heads up. And, obviously, being designed at that period of time, there was no consideration of what we as people might want to do. It's not even a question of the FCC regulation or anything like that for us. The air belongs to everyone who breathes it," commented Kantako about the TRA's decision to put an unlicensed transmitter on the air.[7]

WTRA Signs On

Although it was illegal, the TRA decided to put an FM station on the air using money from a Catholic Campaign for Human Development grant. "We got the equipment . . . for about $600 out of a catalog," said Kantako. They purchased a 1-watt Panaxis transmitter, assembled it themselves, adjusted it for 107.1 MHz so as not to interfere with existing stations, put up the antenna, and made their first broadcast on November 27, 1986, from the living room of Kantako's apartment, which he shared with his wife Dia and their three children, Kanodi, Eboni, and Mbanna, Jr. What we did "goes against what we've been told about radio—that you need to go to college for four years," Kantako said about the group's ability to construct and operate the station.

They named the station for the association, giving it the call letters WTRA. At its inception, about a dozen Hay Homes residents worked on WTRA, whose signal was audible only within a mile and a half of the transmitter. Nevertheless, the micropower station reached most of Springfield's African-American residents.

The TRA also established a 1,000-book library, called the Malcolm X Children's Library, with books purchased at garage sales and used book shops. "We're scavengers," said Townsend of their ability to get things done with almost no money, although "recyclers" seems a more accurate description of their activities. Even the tape recorders and microphones used for the radio station were purchased at garage sales and second-hand stores. Kantako concurred: "The biggest lie that has ever been told is that it costs a lot to run a radio station," refuting the FCC's assertion that broadcasters need to be well-heeled.

Until the tape recorders were purchased, WTRA was on the air for just two nights per week, broadcasting live. In 1988 the station went to three nights per night, twelve hours per night (6:00 p.m. to 6:00 a.m.), carrying commentary, news reports, and music, "mostly reggae and rap music that is not sexist, brutal, or materialistic," said Townsend.[8] The station also changed its name to Zoom Black Magic Liberation Radio to reflect its broader outlook and purpose, which Kantako described as "to build community. We're really trying to raise the consciousness of the people."[9]

Although listened to in the black community, the station was largely ignored by Springfield authorities and the FCC. That changed in 1989, after a police beating hospitalized Johnny Howell, a middle-aged father. Kantako interviewed Howell at the hospital and broadcast the interview with requests that listeners call the station and describe their experiences with police. Many came forward with reports of abuse, which were broadcast with commentaries referring to arrests as "kidnappings" and cops as "pigs" and the "occupying army." During musical interludes, the NWA song, "Fuck the Police," was often played, along with recordings from other militant rappers like Public Enemy. According to Kantako, police were aware of the broadcasts and would tell people complaining of police brutality to "go and tell your radio station" what happened.

In March, the station covered a three-day long standoff between the police and Doug Thomas, whom Kantako had known since his youth. A domestic dispute had escalated until Thomas drew a gun on his girlfriend and mother-in-law, holding them hostage. When the police arrived, they surrounded the house. The next morning, an "occupation army" of 100 "masked men dressed for war" surrounded the house, according to Kantako, who was on the scene, recording events and broadcasting them over the air. On the third day, the police stormed the house. Kantako, with the assistance of people at the scene, reported: "Dougie Thomas is shot . . . Dougie Thomas has been shot. . . . People are running all around the area. . . . We're following the crowd toward the crime scene. . . . We have a full-fledged riot going on here now. Police are jumping on people. The Thomas family is highly upset."

The police announced that Thomas shot the two women and then shot himself, which Kantako disputed. On the air, Kantako asserted that the police were lying about the events, that they had overreacted to a domestic dispute and were responsible for the deaths. He described the large police deployment as a "military death squad."

Around this time, Zoom Black Magic Liberation Radio started rebroadcasting police dispatches so that the community was aware of where the police were and what they were doing. The station also demanded that an independent police review board be established in Springfield. The predominantly white city council held a hearing on this issue and rejected the proposal.

Because of the broadcasts, police brutality in the projects stopped, but harassment of the Kantakos started. The harassment has never ceased. Dia Kantako was arrested and handcuffed in front of a group of children attending the Marcus Garvey School for driving her '77 Pontiac without insurance. Police arrested nine-year-old Mbanna, Jr., for getting into a shoving match at school when he stopped another boy from stomping on his lunch.

The police tried to stop a wiener roast hosted by the Kantakos for children in the Malcolm X Human Rights Club, because they didn't have a campfire permit. "The cops and hook and ladder fire truck backed off when the kids ignored them and continued roasting their wienies and marshmallows," Townsend reported.[10]

Reporters for the *Nation* and the Chicago-based *People's Tribune* visited Kantako for an on-air discussion of police brutality, and as they left they were stopped by the police. "As soon as we left Kantako's apartment, two police officers yelled at us to stop and then ordered us to spread our legs and place our hands against the wall. They had been standing near the apartment next to marked-car units, apparently listening to our on-the-air comments on police terror," reported *Nation* writer Luis Rodriguez. The intimidation stopped twenty minutes later, when project residents confronted the cops after listening to reports of the harassment on the microradio station.[11]

The Springfield police chief complained to the FCC soon after Dougie Thomas's death, claiming that he had received complaints about the station's use of profanity. Responding to the police chief's complaint, FCC agents visited the station on April 6, 1989, and determined that Kantako was operating without a license. He was ordered to stop broadcasting and slapped with a $750 fine, which he refused to pay.

Kantako shut the station down that day, but fired it up again on April 17 during a press conference in which he demanded that the police arrest him for operating the station. When the police refused, Kantako went to the federal building in Springfield, where he asked to be arrested by U.S. marshals, who also refused. As a result of these confrontations, Kantako decided to put the station on twenty-four hours a day, seven days a week, which is how it has operated since.

Soon after, the station was renamed "Black Liberation Radio" to reflect its political outlook. It has since been called African Liberation Radio and Human Rights Radio, reflecting the changing perspective of Kantako and his associates. "We're learning as we go," said Kantako about the changes. "We named our original organization the name that we thought was a solution to our problems—the Tenant's Rights Association. We thought if we got tenant's rights—boom—everything would fall into place. We learned that wasn't the case."[12]

In March 1990 a federal court ordered Kantako to shut down his transmitter. Kantako ignored the order, but he did contact the San Francisco-based National Lawyers Guild's Committee on Democratic Communications (CDC), formed in 1987 to explore "the applicability of traditional First Amendment concepts in the face of the face of the world-wide monopolization of communication resources by commercial interests."[13]

"I got an e-mail from Mike Townsend" said attorney Peter Franck, cochair with Sally Harms of the CDC about their first direct contact with Black Liberation Radio.[14] "We felt what they were doing was very important. The choice was to either reform the existing media or start your own." Franck added that he doubts that the existing corporate-controlled media can be reformed.

After discussing the case, the CDC decided to take on Kantako's case. "This started the ball rolling on legal research on free radio broadcasting," said Franck. Alan Korn, then a law student and the CDC's Legal Research Coordinator, wrote a "Brief on the Constitutional and Human Right to Practice Micro Radio Without

Government Interference," which Kantako and the Guild were prepared to file in the event that the FCC tried to force him off the air again. The brief argued that the FCC's complete ban on microradio stations, adopted in 1978 at the urging of NPR, was unconstitutional.

"We debated whether we should go to court affirmatively to try and get the ban on low-power radio ruled unconstitutional," explained Franck, but "Mbanna wasn't very anxious to go to court. He didn't have much faith in the courts. And our feeling was that going in affirmatively makes it tougher to win than if we are defending him against a criminal charge or action." The brief was never filed on Kantako's behalf because the FCC, having received no complaints about Kantako from commercial broadcasters, decided not to pursue the case. Although the brief wasn't filed, it wasn't wasted—it was later revised and submitted in behalf of Free Radio Berkeley (see Chapter 7).

After going on the air twenty-four hours a day, Black Liberation Radio developed several unique programs, some of which are still broadcast by the station. One, called *Notes on the Devil's News*, is a deconstruction or alternative interpretation of a news event covered that day by the commercial media. The program is typically a half-hour long. Sometimes *Notes on the Devil's News* is a sentence-by-sentence or paragraph-by-paragraph refutation of a news story or newscast; other times it is simply an alternative interpretation of the event.

The purpose of the program is to demonstrate to listeners that news media shape or slant news stories to make authorities appear informed and objective and to make political dissidents or protesters appear ignorant and biased. As Dia Kantako, who does the on-air deconstruction, points out, news reporters use terms such as "rampage" to describe the actions of youth who actually "rose in defense of our community."[15]

Another program, *Brothers at the Real Table*, is a live talk show moderated by Kantako, featuring interviews with guests such as authors Zears Miles and Terrance Jackson or reporter Luis Rodriquez. The interviews are usually conducted by telephone and amplified using a twenty-dollar speaker phone. When guests visit Black Liberation Radio in person, they are usually invited to participate in the "Real Table" discussions in Kantako's living room around a kitchen table, which is how the program got its name. The interviews are taped and rebroadcast later in the day or the next morning.

Good White Sources airs daily from noon to 2:00 p.m. and features taped presentations by white critics of corporate capitalism, such as Noam Chomsky and Barbara Ehrenreich. The tapes are sent to the station by alternative program suppliers, such as Radio Free Maine (see Chapter 9).

Although Black Liberation Radio, now called Human Rights Radio, continues to broadcast, its primary listeners, the residents of the Hay Homes project, have been uprooted. The Springfield Housing Authority decided in 1995 to close the project and evict the remaining residents, including the Kantako family.

According to Townsend, "the property is now too valuable to keep as low income housing." Hotels and offices have been built nearby, and the city wants a middle-income housing development built on the Hay Homes site.

After learning of the eviction plans, Kantako vowed to fight them, promising that he would stay in the projects until they were torn down. True to his word, Kantako started a new radio program, *The Great Land Grab,* which decried the "Negro Removal Program" inaugurated by the housing authority, and he stayed in his apartment as other families, lured by federal housing vouchers and pie-in-the-sky promises of better housing, moved out. By mid-1996, the Hay Homes project was nearly vacant and the once well-tended garden plots were filled with weeds. By the end of 1997, nearly all the apartments, except that of Mbanna and Dia Kantako, were boarded up and vacant, but Human Rights Radio nevertheless remained on the air.

In February 1997 the Springfield Housing Authority filed an eviction suit against Kantako, claiming that he owed nearly $3,000 in back rent. After a judge ruled that he move or be moved out by noon, March 3, Kantako left the apartment and moved to a new one with Dia and their children.[16] "Mbanna was off the air for just about ninety minutes during the move," said Mike Townsend.

Decatur's Black Liberation Radio

The first station inspired by Kantako's example and the second micropower station to take to the air was Black Liberation Radio of Decatur, Illinois. Like Springfield, which is forty miles west, Decatur is a predominantly white city with an entrenched white power structure that perpetuates itself through at-large elections, ties to business, and a police force that doesn't hesitate to use brute force against political dissidents, minorities, and union workers, as demonstrated during the Caterpillar, Bridgestone, and Staley strikes.[17]

Started by Napoleon Williams and Mildred Jones on August 20, 1990, Black Liberation Radio broadcast from a studio in the couple's small west-side home using a less-than-one-watt Panaxis transmitter tuned to 107.3 MHz FM, a vacant frequency in the Decatur-Springfield radio market. The station was created to give Decatur's African-American community uncensored access to the airwaves. A leaflet distributed in the African-American community to announce its sign-on reported that Black Liberation Radio would give "a voice to those who have no voice of their own through the mass media."[18]

"We want total community involvement, so anybody can be one the air," said Williams about the station's philosophy. "If you have a problem with the judicial system, you don't have to call Napoleon Williams and ask him, 'What can you do?' You can come on and present your case to the people. There may be someone out there that will hear you, who has had the same problem and knows what to do."[19]

In Williams's view, radio should operate like public access channels on cable television, where interested groups and individuals can produce and air programs.

Two weeks after Black Liberation Radio signed on—and started criticizing Macon County states attorney Lawrence Fichter for herding African-Americans through the judicial system like slaves through a plantation-era auction—Williams and Jones learned firsthand how justice was dispensed in Decatur. The couple had their house raided by police, were repeatedly arrested and jailed, and even lost custody of their daughter, Unique Dream. A journalist at the *Decatur Herald & Tribune,* the city's daily newspaper, acknowledged that the arrests and harassment give "the appearance [the states attorney and police] are out to silence him [Williams]. That's very obvious."[20] An African-American newspaper put it more bluntly, describing the actions as a "harassment campaign" waged by "a white states attorney."[21]

Then Williams was charged with fondling his ten-year-old daughter, whom he fathered with another woman. The *Nation* reported that "there was uncertain evidence even according to the prosecutors, [so the charge] was reduced to battery on a plea bargain offered by Williams himself in exchange for release from prison and recovery of possessions confiscated when police invaded his home."[22]

The next bizarre encounter occurred several weeks later, when Fichter asserted that Williams was hired to videotape the issuing of a gang contract for the killing of two narcotics officers. To get the videotape, members of the Police Emergency Response Team conducted a late-night, guns-drawn, battering ram invasion of the Williams's home on October 13, 1990, two months after Black Liberation Radio signed on. The videotape was not found because it apparently never existed, but police did find several others, including some Mickey Mouse cartoons and some home videos of Christmas and family reunions, which they seized, watched at the station with Fichter, and later returned.

Shortly after that, the station was visited by the FCC, which ordered Williams to stop broadcasting and slapped him with a $17,500 fine. "I told them if I got $17,500, come and get it . . . Hell, if I had $17,500, I'd have a better radio station than this," said Williams, who ignored the agency and continued to broadcast. He has not heard from them since then, adding, "They're the least of my problems."

Jones's descent into a Kafkaesque hell began in December 1991, when police responded to a neighbor's call about a dispute between Williams and Jones. When the police arrived, Jones told them she did not make the call and did not need them. Nevertheless, the cops arrested Williams. The states attorney, still embarrassed by the late-night seizure of the Mickey Mouse cartoons, decided to prosecute Williams and convened a grand jury, where he demanded that Jones testify against Williams. She refused. Because of her refusal, Jones was sentenced to jail for contempt of court.

While Jones was in jail, a herd of cops and family services personnel stampeded into Williams's and Jones's home to seize Unique Dream, claiming that Williams was unfit to take care of his own daughter. The court's claim was based on the sexual misconduct charge filed against Williams, which had been dropped. As the authorities were snatching his daughter, Williams went on the air, telling listeners, "They've kidnapped my daughter."

Unique Dream was then made a ward of the court and placed with her grandmother. Throughout this nightmare, Williams, with help from a cadre of volunteers, managed to keep Black Liberation Radio on the air, informing listeners about the new twists in a very twisted case.

When freed from jail on the contempt charge in April 1992, Jones went to court to get back custody of Unique Dream, but rather than getting the child, she was arrested at the courthouse with Williams for criminal trespassing. Williams was beaten by the police and also charged with aggravated assault on a cop.

Frustrated, Jones brought Unique Dream home from her grandmother's house in May without first getting the court's permission. For this, Jones was arrested for child abduction. At the time of Jones's arrest, the court again seized—"kidnapped" is perhaps a more accurate word—Unique Dream and has since then prevented Jones and Williams from seeing her. One reason given by States Attorney Fichter for refusing to let Jones and Williams visit their daughter is "that the children's safety is at risk, that Napoleon Williams is utilizing the children as pawns in his egregious conduct to and toward lawful authorities."[23] In other words, their daughter has been taken from them because Williams refuses to obey what he views as discriminatory laws.

Fichter's contention "that the children's safety is at risk" is not supported by Kevin Kehoe, an attorney appointed by the court to represent the children. "I found Napoleon to be bright and Mildred to be very nice," said Kehoe. "My recommendation was to return the kids to Napoleon and Mildred."[24]

The problem stems from Fichter and the Department of Child and Family Services, who, according to Kehoe, want Williams and Jones "to jump through hoops. . . . That's what bothers me the most. You or I would say, 'We'd jump through the hoop and get our kids back.' Here's a man who won't bow down." Kehoe eventually filed a motion with the court asking that Fichter be replaced by a special prosecutor, but his motion was denied.

To protest the state's abduction of the child, a Unique Dream Defense Committee was formed, which also protested the charges against Jones. "They've been taking African kids away from their families dating back to the days of slavery," said Mary Johnson, speaking at a defense committee protest in Decatur. "They got my son, too. But I've decided that, even if I have to give that son up, I'm going to fight for my people. It's not about me; it's about us and ours."[25] Her speech was recorded and broadcast over Black Liberation Radio, as were other speeches at this and many other demonstrations.

Throughout the jailings and harassment, Williams and Jones tried to keep Black Liberation Radio on the air, but it fell silent in 1994, when Williams and Jones were in jail for offenses stemming from their attempts to get Unique Dream back. Williams wound up serving fourteen months for the incident at the courthouse, and Jones was jailed for violating probation, which she was given for taking Unique Dream back home. Consequently, Black Liberation Radio was silent during most of the labor actions at Staley, Caterpillar, and Bridgestone, where police beat strikers and used pepper spray on them. As Williams remarked about this brutality, "People learned that I wasn't just a nut yelling about the police."

When released, Williams immediately put Black Liberation Radio back on 107.3 FM, printed and distributed leaflets announcing the return of the station, and invited listeners to participate in program production. "Let's say you disagree with me. All you need to do is make a tape. I'll play it for everybody," said Williams, who loans out tape recorders to prospective programmers. "If you came by, we can make you an on-the-spot reporter."

Williams described responses to his offer: "We've got guys that bring by tapes. I had a brother who bought a three-cassette tape of Malcolm X and brought it by here, who said, 'As soon as I saw this for sale, I knew you might want it.'"

Black Liberation Radio does not have a specific schedule during the week; only a few hours daily are devoted to scheduled programs. Most mornings, Williams does a show similar to *Notes on the Devil's News,* where he discusses and reinterprets news stories reported that day by the corporate press. "A lot of people don't buy the newspaper because they know Napoleon's going over it," said Jones about the show. The show is taped live and rebroadcast later in the day.

After that, the station often plays music, sometimes with Jones as disc jockey. On some nights a live call-in show, *Hot Line,* is featured. Music programs by disc jockeys such as D.J. Ice also air on weekdays. About the schedule, Williams said, "Throughout the day, you're going to find something you dislike and then, if you listen long enough, something you're going to like—that's guaranteed."

On Saturdays there is *Blunt Sessions,* a talk show on current issues, and *Black Education Enrichment Forum* (BEEF), which addresses such topics as Black male-female relationships. "Most of our programming is directed to a younger audience. We want to build some fighters. We want to introduce some people back to the struggle—we want to teach them what we did in the '60s, in the '70s. We want to teach them how to protest again," said Williams about the programming.

However, not all of the programs are directed to young people. Every Wednesday night the station carries *Way Back Wednesdays,* a music show featuring older rhythm and blues hits, which are taped by deejay Ron Skeet. On Sundays, Black Liberation Radio features religious and spiritual programming, including a gospel music show recorded by "Big Tom" and sermons by Louis Farrakhan and other African-American religious leaders. "Sunday is religious programming," Williams explained, "No cursing, rap, or anything like that."

In May 1996 a commercial, album-oriented rock station in a nearby city signed onto 107.3 MHz, forcing Black Liberation Radio to change frequencies. Because he needed to shut down the station to alter its frequency, Williams decided it might be a good idea to install a new, more powerful transmitter at that time.

To buy a new transmitter, Williams conducted a one-day fundraiser over the air, asking listeners to drop five dollars off on Saturday. Very late on Friday, Williams heard a knock on the door. When opened, there stood a local gang member who said, "I'm going to pay for twenty brothers right now," and handed Williams $100. During the next twenty-four hours, Williams was given more than $1,000, almost all of it in $5.00 donations.

The money was enough to buy a 15-watt transmitter, a new antenna, and even a meter to check the transmitter's output. The new transmitter allowed Black Liberation Radio to broadcast on 107.7 MHz to most of Decatur, rather than just its east or west sides. "This station really does belong to the people," said Williams about the response to the fundraiser.

The new transmitter didn't serve the people very long, however. On January 9, 1997, the home of Williams and Jones was again raided by the police, who had a search warrant allowing them to seize electronic equipment that could be used for "eavesdropping."[26] The allegations were not contained in the search warrant, but they include the allegation that Williams taped his conversations with public officials without getting their permission, which is a felony in Illinois. (In most states, this taping is legal.) Rather than seizing tapes and tape recorders, the police seized every piece of broadcasting equipment in the house, which suggests that the raid was an attempt to force Black Liberation Radio off the air.

After news about the raid got out, Black Liberation Radio received help in getting back on the air from many sources. Money, tapes, and tape recorders were brought to the station by Decatur supporters, and Stephen Dunifer, founder of Free Radio Berkeley, sent Williams a new transmitter. With this help, Black Liberation Radio was back on the air in a few weeks.

As Williams was rebuilding the station, Attorney General Jim Ryan was convening a grand jury in Macon County, apparently with the assistance of Fichter.[27] The grand jury indicted Williams for eavesdropping on April 7, and a warrant for his arrest was issued. Aware of what was happening, Williams moved the station to a nearby house, where it would be safe. As a consequence, when police battered in the front door of Williams's and Jones's home on May 10, the station remained on the air, providing reports about the couple's arrest. Williams was arrested on the eavesdropping charges and Jones was arrested for concealing and aiding a fugitive. Williams was later released on bond and is awaiting trial, but Jones remains in jail; her three-year probation for a shoplifting charge was revoked.

The Revolution Spreads

Williams's belief that radio stations should function like public access channels, rather than as producers of pablum and profits, is also held by Tom Reveille, who in 1991 started Radio Free Venice, California's first micropower station. "In my view, we have a media government. If you need information, you can only get it from the media. They control the elections. They have a stranglehold on information," Reveille said about the corporate media, which dominate the U.S. airwaves. "This is the only war in history where one side gets all of its information from the other side."[28]

Inspired by the example of Mbanna Kantako, Reveille decided to break the media's information stranglehold by starting a free station, where listeners could become program producers. "It was open to the community on an equal basis. It was quite a heterogeneous mixture of people on the air," he said. The station was open about its location and provided its telephone number to listeners. For a studio, Reveille used the enclosed porch on the house where he lived, so that passersby could see the studio and come in and talk, if they so wished.

The FCC took advantage of the station's openness. On May 29, 1991, FCC agents, backed by Los Angeles cops, showed up at Reveille's door and informed him that he was breaking the law. Reveille responded that they were not violating the law because Congress gave the FCC jurisdiction over interstate and foreign communications, not microradio, where signals barely travel two miles. The police responded by grabbing and handcuffing him. They then uncuffed him and left.

Despite the FCC visit, Radio Free Venice remained on the air. Reveille explained his decision to continue broadcasting: "What was important was [not] the station, but to challenge the FCC." The FCC responded to the challenge on November 13, when two agents and four federal marshals invaded Reveille's residence with guns drawn. When one of Reveille's roommates came downstairs to see what the commotion was all about, a marshal aimed his gun at her and warned her not to move. "They ransacked the rooms of people who had nothing to do with the station," Reveille said about the raid. "They didn't take the antenna, [but] they took cash, videotapes, 160 audiotapes, files—everything they damn well pleased." Reveille never got the equipment or his personal possessions back, and the station never returned to the air.

As the FCC was silencing Radio Free Venice, another free station calling itself KAPW signed on in Phoenix, Arizona, the heart of the Goldwater state. The station was operated by Bill Dougan on 88.9 MHz from his home. Unlike Tom Reveille, a politically dedicated libertarian, Dougan was not involved in political activities before getting involved in radio. He had written a few letters to the editor about assault rifles and J. Edgar Hoover, but not much more. This changed in 1988 when commercial station KFYI-FM dropped talk show host Tom Leykis, to whom Dougan had listened almost daily. To get Leykis back on the air, Dougan initiated a boycott of KFYI advertisers; the station responded by suing Dougan for interfering with their business. Faced with the expenses of defending himself from KFYI's harassment suit, Dougan called off the boycott.[29]

The experience left Dougan disenchanted with commercial radio, so he decided to put on a noncommercial station, which he dubbed "Arizona's Most

Controversial Station." KAPW aired a variety of materials, including tapes of "controversial" speakers like Madalyn Murray O'Hair, Native American music, and public affairs shows—but not for long. On March 12, 1992, FCC agents showed up at Dougan's door, asking to see the transmitter. He refused to allow the agents in—or so the FCC says—but he did invite in representatives of the news media, who had gathered outside his home. The FCC responded by fining Dougan.[30]

Dougan shut down his station, but appealed the fine in the U.S. Ninth Circuit Court of Appeals, where he argued that the FCC's restrictions on low-power broadcasting were unconstitutional. The CDC filed a friend-of-the-court brief in that case, based largely on the research that they had done for Mbanna Kantako, but the court did not reach a decision, ruling instead that the proper jurisdiction for the case was federal district court.[31]

Dougan returned to the air in December 1994 after Radio Free Berkeley, defended by the CDC, beat back FCC attempts to silence that station. Dougan's new station, called KAFR or Arizona Free Radio, was created as "a refreshing change from far-right hate radio," carrying many of the same program types that appeared earlier on Free Radio Berkeley—a gay and lesbian show, women's programs, and punk rock music.[32]

Two other stations inspired by Mbanna Kantako's example were Radio Free Detroit and Black Liberation Radio 2, which broadcast to Richmond, Virginia. Radio Free Detroit, although inspired by Zoom Black Magic Liberation Radio, differed from its model in several ways: The station was secretive about its location and sponsorship, never recruited citizens to produce programs or otherwise participate in the station's operations, and never directly challenged the FCC, as Kantako, Williams, and Reveille had. Instead of opening the station to the public, all of the programming was produced by "the RFD collective."

Radio Free Detroit broadcast just two days per week—on Sundays from 3:00 p.m. to 1:00 a.m. and Thursdays from 6:30 p.m. to 1:00 p.m.—for a few months at the end of 1991 and the beginning of 1992. The station broadcast on 106.3 MHz, near the top of the FM band. The FCC apparently learned about the station from an article in the *Fifth Estate*, Detroit's alternative weekly newspaper. When the FCC showed up at the operators' door, accompanied by a few cops and a television crew trying to do a story on the station, Radio Free Detroit was silenced. "The collective took the station off the airwaves that night to save the equipment," reported Larry Talbot, a member of the collective.[33] The station has made a few broadcasts since the 1992 sign-off, but its sporadic operation has kept it from developing an audience.

Black Liberation Radio 2 was on the air between December 29, 1994, and June 25, 1995. The station was started by Jahi Kubweza, who became "tired of being bombarded by lies. So we took it upon ourselves to show the difference between the information being made available and the information withheld."[34] Black

Liberation Radio 2 featured programs on economics, government, health, and a host of other issues, along with poetry, rap, reggae, jazz, and instrumental music. It directly challenged the FCC by operating on 91.7 MHz, twenty-four hours per day, seven days per week, with 30 watts of power.

FCC agents paid the station a visit on December 29 and asked to see the transmitter. "I made a mistake," Kubweza said about his decision to allow the agents in. Once in, they seized the transmitter, the antenna, and all other electronic equipment that was visible—even equipment that had nothing to do with the station. Kubweza said that he learned a major lesson from his mistake: Never allow FCC agents onto the premises.

Although the FCC believed that it could stop the growing micropower radio revolution by issuing fines and seizing a few transmitters, it was wrong. Emboldened by the success of Kantako and Williams and angered by the harassment of Kubweza and other micropower broadcasters, even more free radio broadcasters took to the air.

NOTES

1. Mike Townsend, in person interview by author, July 8, 1996.

2. Ibid.

3. Quoted in Steven Shields and Robert Ogles, "Black Liberation Radio: A Case Study of Free-Micro-broadcasting," *Howard Journal of Communication* 5: 173–183.

4. Mbanna Kantako, quoted in Sharon Albert-Honore, "Empowering Voices: KUCB and Black Liberation Radio," in *Mediated Messages and African-American Culture* (Thousand Oaks, Calif.: Sage, 1996), p. 208.

5. John Fiske, *Media Matters* (Minneapolis: University of Minnesota Press, 1994), p. 228.

6. David Burke, "'I'm Still Saying, Can You Hear Me?" *Decatur Herald & Review,* January 12, 1997, p. A4.

7. Quoted in Steve LaBlanc, "Revolution Radio," *Version 90*, p. 21.

8. Sheila Nopper, "Unleashed: Micropower Radio Claims Airwave Access," *Word* (Canada), April 1996, p. 29.

9. Eric Harrison, "Out of the Night," *Los Angeles Times,* November 19, 1990, p. E1.

10. Mike Townsend, "Memo on Black Liberation Radio," June 27, 1996.

11. Luis Rodriguez, "Rappin' in the Hood," *Nation,* August 12/19, 1991, pp. 192–194.

12. Mbanna Kantako, interview by author, July 8, 1996.

13. "The National Lawyers Guild's Committee on Democratic Communications," online posting, available from: <http://www.surf.com/~graham/microradio.answer.html>.

14. Peter Franck, in person interview by author, March 5, 1997.

15. For an in-depth discussion of Dia's method of deconstructing news stories, see Fiske, *Media Matters.*

16. Lisa Kernek, "Outlaw DJ Ordered Out of Hay Homes," *Springfield Journal-Register,* February 26, 1997, p. 9; Lisa Kernek, "Move Doesn't Silence Pirate Radio Operator in Hay Homes," *Springfield Journal Register,* March 4, 1997, p. 2; Sheila Nopper, "Kantako Breaks the Silence," *Illinois Times,* March 6–12, 1997.

17. See "Police Put Down Union Protests," *Chicago Sun Times,* June 26, 1994, p. 27; Stephen Franklin, "A City Divided—Us Vs. Them," *Chicago Tribune,* June 24, 1994, Business section, p. 1.

18. Leaflet for "Black Liberation Radio, Decatur, 107.3 FM," undated.

19. Napoleon Williams, interview by author, July 9, 1996. Unless otherwise identified, all subsequent remarks by Napoleon Williams are from this interview.

20. In person interview, May 12, 1997. The journalist, an editor, asked not to be identified.

21. Richard Muhammad, "Black Couple Fights for their Child," *Final Call,* November 24, 1993, p. 5.

22. Rodriguez, "Rappin' in the Hood."

23. Quoted in Dave Moore and Billy Tyus, "The Voice of 'Liberation,'" *Decatur Herald Review,* January 12, 1997, p. A5.

24. Kevin Kehoe, telephone interview by author, May 12, 1997.

25. For a more detailed account of William's and Jones's problems with the police and court system, see Muhammad, "Black Couple Fights for Their Child"; "Free Mildred Jones," *People's Tribune,* March 3, 1992, p. 7; and Anthony Prince, "Napoleon Williams: A Rebel Broadcaster Speaks Out," *People's Tribune,* April 1996, p. 11.

26. "Search Warrant in the Circuit Court for the Sixth Judicial Circuit of Illinois, Macon County," January 7, 1997.

27. Since grand jury proceedings are closed, it is difficult to ascertain what goes on in the jury room, and in this case in particular prosecutors have been particularly close-lipped.

28. Tom Reveille, telephone interview by author, December 27, 1996. Unless otherwise identified, all subsequent remarks by Tom Reveille are from this interview.

29. Dennis Wagner, "He's Back: Radio Pirate on a Mission," *Phoenix Gazette,* December 19, 1994, p. A1.

30. "In the Matter of William Leigh Dougan," *11 FCC Rcd 12154* (May 28, 1996).

31. *William Leigh Dougan v. FCC,* United States Court of Appeals, *75 Rad. Reg. 2nd* (P & F) *214* (April 20, 1994).

32. Julie Newberg, "Neighborhood Station Challenges Regulators, Right-Wing Programs," *Arizona Republic,* April 24, 1995, p. C5.

33. Letter from "Friends of Radio Free Detroit," April 7, 1992.

34. Jahi Kubweza, telephone interview by author, January 2, 1996.

7

The Free Radio Revolution:
Free Radio Berkeley and the
West Coast Revolt

Berkeley and San Francisco, birthplaces of the Beat movement of the 1950s and the free speech and counterculture movements of the 1960s, became the center of the microradio revolution around 1993. The free radio revolution shifted to the San Francisco Bay Area, where the National Lawyers Guild's Committee on Democratic Communications (CDC) was based, where the protests to Save KPFA were getting off the ground (see Chapter 4), and where Stephen Dunifer, a former broadcast engineer for commercial radio and television stations, lived. Dunifer started Free Radio Berkeley as a direct challenge to the FCC's ban on low-power broadcasting and as a laboratory for developing and distributing a low-cost micropower transmitter that could be used by community groups and citizen activists.

The Beginning

Prior to putting Free Radio Berkeley on the air, Dunifer designed and tested several homemade FM transmitters in his workshop-home above an electronics repair store in West Berkeley. Dunifer's residence consisted of two bedrooms, a living room, and a workshop larger than all the other rooms combined. In the workshop, Dunifer pared his prototype FM transmitters down to one that was small, portable, stable, and inexpensive.

At a Save KPFA protest outside of KPFA's Berkeley studio in February 1993, Dunifer unveiled his new portable FM transmitter. Dunifer fired up the shoe-box sized portable transmitter and passed the mike around to protestors, who voiced their opposition to Pacifica's new policies. The purpose of the broadcast was to show Pacifica's bosses what real community radio was all about.

Two months later, Dunifer began broadcasting on Sunday nights between nine and ten o'clock from his workshop-home, announcing, "This is Free Radio Berkeley, 88.1 on your FM dial." Shortly after Free Radio Berkeley signed on, San Francisco–based FCC agents monitored the 15-watt broadcasts, which denounced the FCC for promoting corporate interests rather than the public interest, an issue that Dunifer has hammered at consistently.[1] "We are attempting to redress a greater wrong that is essentially a theft of the people's airwaves by corporate interests that have hijacked the whole thing," Dunifer said about his operation of an unlicensed station.

Surprised and angered by the broadcasts, an agent from the FCC's Compliance and Information Bureau in San Francisco loaded direction-finding equipment into his car on April 23, 1993, and travelled to Berkeley, where the free station's "signals were isolated by the agent to the vicinity of 6th Street and Alliston Way."[2] A week later, several agents returned to Berkeley, where they parked and waited for the station to return to the air. At 9:00 p.m. as usual, Free Radio Berkeley signed on. When the transmissions began, the agents turned on their "close-in direction-finding equipment" and locked onto the transmissions originating from Dunifer's workshop-home, which they identified as the source of the "distasteful" unlicensed messages.

At 9:55 p.m., one of the agents knocked on Dunifer's door and asked if he could inspect the station's transmitter. The agent claimed that U.S. laws allowed him to inspect any transmitter operating within the United States. Dunifer refused to open his door, and the befuddled agent went back to his car, where he and his cohorts waited to see what would happen next. A short time later, the agents noticed a long-haired, bearded fellow wearing wire-rimmed glasses leave the premises. One of the agents accosted the fellow, who refused to identify himself. The agents later identified him as Stephen Paul Dunifer, a Berkeley anarchist and radical activist.

Dunifer said that he expected the visit from the FCC. One reason for going on the air was to challenge the FCC rules prohibiting micropower broadcasting, but before the rules could be challenged in court, he had to be cited by the FCC. "The first broadcasts were made from a fixed location to get the attention of the FCC," Dunifer said. The broadcasts were "an absolute attempt to challenge directly the FCC's regulatory structure and policies. Based on the work of the National Lawyer Guild's Committee on Democratic Communications [in the Kantako case], I felt sure we had a very solid legal basis to proceed on if we could find a proper venue."[3]

However, once the FCC identified Dunifer's workshop-home as the source of the broadcasts, the "station went mobile," operating that way for a year and a half until the end of 1994. "The transmitters were put into backpacks along with other portable studio equipment and were all hiked up into the hills of Berkeley," Dunifer reports. A battery was lugged along to provide electrical power for the transmitter, which went on the air Sundays from 9:00 p.m. to midnight, airing tapes made by community groups, local bands, and even interviews. "We are carrying out the original mission and intent of what radio should be in this country, and that is a community-driven local operation that is assessable to anyone."

There were several strategic reasons for going mobile. The first was to protect Dunifer's residence from being raided by the FCC. As long as the station was not broadcasting from the residence, the FCC could not get a search warrant to enter the residence and seize broadcasting equipment, which by this time was piled high in the workshop. The second was to make it difficult for the FCC to locate and stop the broadcasts.

The strategy worked, but it angered Bay Area broadcasters and irate FCC officials, who continued to monitor Free Radio Berkeley's broadcasts. When the infuriated FCC agents served a Notice of Apparent Liability on Dunifer on June 1, telling him that Free Radio Berkeley had been monitored broadcasting from his residence on April 25 and May 2, they levied a whopping $20,000 fine, rather than the $1,000 fine called for by their own regulations. [4]

Louis ("Luke") Hiken, a San Francisco attorney and member of the CDC, drafted Dunifer's response to the Notice of Apparent Liability. The response noted that the FCC's fine was "grossly disproportionate to the alleged violations . . . and exceeds the maximum set by statute." Moreover, the response laid out the arguments that would later be raised in U.S. District Court, where the FCC tried to get an injunction to stop Dunifer from broadcasting. It noted that FCC policies were developed "before the advent of FM broadcasting" and "failed to keep pace with . . . technological advances" such as highly stable, low-power FM transmitters, which provide poor people, rather than just large corporations, with access to the broadcasting spectrum. Hiken's response also described the FCC's ban on low-power broadcasting as illegal, observing that the "FCC is constitutionally required to develop a regulatory procedure appropriate to the medium rather than simply creating and enforcing a complete and absolute prohibition on micro-radio."[5]

The FCC officials, of course, rejected all of these arguments on November 8, 1993, explaining that they had the sole power to determine the public interest. They also contended that the $1,000 fine established in 1990 was for "routine" cases, which they did not consider this to be. The whopping fine was issued, they disclosed, because they considered Dunifer to be "a recalcitrant individual who decide[d] to willfully operate a radio transmitter without the required authorization, as a protest against the regulatory power of the Commission." Their proof of Dunifer's recalcitrance was that they had repeatedly monitored the mobile Free Radio Berkeley, even though they could not locate the station's transmitter. In response, Hiken filed an appeal called an Application for Review in Washington, D.C., on December 2.

Besides getting the National Lawyers Guild to represent him, Dunifer did several things that the FCC did not expect: He made his case public, began showing others how they could start their own radio stations, and continued to broadcast. To publicize his case, Dunifer sent press releases to alternative, local, and national media and made himself available for interviews, hoping that some journalists would accurately report on his situation. The first stories about Dunifer appeared in Bay Area newspapers, including the *San Francisco Chronicle,* which reported that Dunifer and his colleagues were "encouraging other people" to start up stations. "They offer free workshops on how to build miniature radio stations for less than $200."[6]

Nationally syndicated columnists Alexander Cockburn and Norman Solomon also took up Dunifer's cause.[7] Stories about Free Radio Berkeley also appeared on the Cable News Network (CNN) and in the *New York Times,* but what really garnered publicity for the station was the FBI's inept attempt to link Bay Area radicals to the Unabomber. According to the FBI, an anonymous tipster identified Dunifer as the Unabomber, and an FBI agent decided to pay Dunifer a visit. As a result of the FBI visit, Dunifer's fight with the FCC was described in the *Washington Post,* the *Los Angeles Times,* and other large daily newspapers.[8]

To the chagrin of the FCC, Dunifer began teaching others how to start micropower FM stations, and he started building, advertising, and selling low-power FM transmitters. In May 1993 another Bay Area micropower FM station, San Francisco Liberation Radio (SFLR), appeared on 93.7 MHz. Started by activists Jo Swanson and Richard Edmondson, the station followed in the footsteps of Radio Free Berkeley, becoming mobile. During its initial months of operation, the station broadcast from different locations, hoping to avoid being tracked and silenced by the FCC. Rather than broadcasting just one night a week as Free Radio Berkeley did, SFLR was on two nights, Wednesday and Saturdays, from eight to ten o'clock.

San Francisco–based FCC agents tried to track down SFLR and serve its operators a Notice of Apparent Liability, too, but the station was able to stay one step in front of them for nearly four months. On September 22 FCC agent David Doon finally located what he believed were SFLR transmissions and confronted Edmondson about the broadcasts. Edmondson refused to identify himself to Doon. Frustrated, Doon called the San Francisco police for assistance, and they sent a battalion of police to stop Edmondson's "getaway" car. "There were so many cops out there, I thought I was right in the middle of a riot zone. To think they were all there because of me is a little mind-boggling," said Edmondson about being stopped. He said that the police "were mad that they were being called out for something so insignificant" as a 30-watt radio broadcast.[9]

After learning Edmondson's identity, the FCC issued him a Notice of Apparent Liability imposing a $10,000 fine. Edmondson, like Dunifer, turned to Luke Hiken for legal assistance and then kept on broadcasting.[10]

The FCC Inaction

Rather than quickly denying Dunifer's Application for Review, which would have allowed Hiken to appeal the denial in court, the agency took a different approach, which it hoped would keep Free Radio Berkeley from raising issues about the constitutionality of FCC policies. The FCC let the Application for Review languish in Washington, D.C., for ten months, and then filed in U.S. District Court in California for an injunction ordering Dunifer to stop broadcasting. The FCC reasoned that if it received the injunction, Dunifer could be cited for violating the court order when he broadcast, rather than for violating FCC regulations, thus avoiding the constitutional challenges to its rules.

The FCC hoped that the strategy would allow it to avoid discussing its corporate-pandering policies, but the strategy backfired, largely because of the FCC's duplicity. When the FCC filed in federal district court for the permanent injunction, it also asked for an immediate preliminary injunction, claiming that Free Radio Berkeley's continued operation produced "immediate and irreparable harm." To this argument, Hiken responded that the station had been on for eighteen months, but the FCC was only now seeking an injunction. "Why did they wait for over 18 months to bring it to this court's attention?" Hiken asked.[11] During the eighteen months, the FCC had repeatedly monitored the station, he pointed out, and had only discovered two instances where the free station's signal interfered with other broadcast signals, and in one of these instances the interference was actually caused by the FCC. Although the FCC alleged that Dunifer's transmitter was "likely to emit spurious signals" that could interfere with air navigation, the agency never discovered an instance where it did, suggesting that the agency's argument was fraudulent and disingenuous.

Hiken also pointed out that other low-power stations were on the air, such Black Liberation Radio in Springfield, Illinois, but that the FCC had not sought injunctions to shut them down. "If there is an emergency, why is it they haven't done anything about that [station]? There's no emergency in this case," he said.[12]

Lastly, the FCC claimed that there was no need for the court to discuss any issues except whether Dunifer was operating Free Radio Berkeley without a license, and that the constitutional issues raised by Dunifer should be addressed by the FCC, not the courts. Hiken responded that the "myriad of constitutional violations . . . which arise as a result of the FCC's decision to preclude the poor from having any access to the airwaves must not be sanctioned by this court. There are numerous less restrictive alternatives to the current licensing scheme enforced by the FCC that would provide the American people with use of the airwaves."[13]

Hiken also noted that the FCC in Washington had been sitting on Dunifer's appeal for a year and had not yet ruled on it. If the FCC believed that Free Radio Berkeley presented such a threat to the public interest, it should have acted on the appeal, he reasoned.

The FCC's failure to act on Dunifer's Application for Review gave him time to build more transmitters, which were eagerly grabbed up by activists around the country. In San Francisco's Mission District, Radio Libre signed on during the summer of 1994 using a Dunifer-built transmitter. Started by a group of Latino homeboys and white anarchists on 103.3 MHz, the station broadcasts music, political commentary, and Latino community news and information. The station opened "an avenue of expression for Mission residents," said Ariel, a Latino college student who read anti-Proposition 187 poetry over the air during the November 1994 election. The proposition, which passed, denied undocumented aliens access to social services, including health care and schooling. "It's one thing to say a man can own land," the poet said about Radio Libre's operating without a license. "It's another to say someone owns vibrations going through the air."[14]

Radio Libre has served as a voice unifying the white and Latin residents of the Mission District, according to station listeners and volunteers. "We offer an alternative, a different point of view from what you get in the mainstream media," said Chilango, who plays Latin rhythms interspersed with political talk on his *Sachrichingo Show*.[15] Disc jockey "Velez," by contrast, plays oldies on his *Cruise Night Forever* show, which attracts Latin and white listeners. "Here we are, a bunch of homeboys in the Mission, and we're dedicating our show to Elvis Presley," said Velez.

The FCC's response is that Velez, Chilango, and Ariel were law breakers who must be stopped. In October, FCC agents knocked on the door of the station, demanding to inspect the transmitter, but were turned away because they did not have a search warrant. Feeling heat from their landlord because of the FCC visit and fearing that the agents would return, Radio Libre quickly packed up and moved to another location, from where it has operated sporadically.

In Phoenix, Bill Dougan, emboldened by Dunifer's continuous operation, put Arizona Free Radio back on to the air, saying, "I do want to make a federal case out of it, literally. This is a potential Supreme Court case."[16] In December 1994, Black Liberation 2 took to the airwaves in Virginia. Four months later, Free Radio Santa Cruz went on the air, broadcasting from another Dunifer-built transmitter. Commenting on the sudden growth of free radio stations, Luke Hiken said, "I think this is going to get beyond the ability of the FCC to control, judging from the snowballing of people interested in setting up stations."

That December, as legal arguments were being made in federal court by Luke Hiken and FCC attorneys, Dunifer was invited to move his transmitter from the Berkeley hills to the home of punk rock musician John Benson in North Oakland. Wanting "to get out of the weather," Dunifer "set up operations in a ripped out bathroom" on the second floor of the home, a group-living space that had housed radical activists and counterculturalists since the '60s. The already recognizable house, painted pink with a huge green frog sculpture in front, soon became the symbol of Free Radio Berkeley.

The FCC at a Loss

Judge Claudia Wilken of the federal district court stunned the FCC on January 20, 1995, when she ruled that its request "for a temporary injunction is hereby denied." The FCC's hope that it could avoid addressing the constitutionality of its ban on low-power broadcasting were further dashed when Judge Wilken ruled that "the FCC is arguably violating its statutory mandate as well as the First Amendment by refusing" to reconsider its rules on microradio. Based on the evidence, she also concluded that "the record does not support the . . . assertion [that] because Defendant's equipment is not FCC-approved, it must be considered likely to emit spurious signals without a warning."[17]

The decision so stunned FCC attorney David Silberman that he insultingly babbled the following to Judge Wilken:

> Your Honor, this opens up such a can of worms. You don't realize. I mean it. Your Honor, what would happen would be that you've given carte blanche to this group of people who think they can operate a radio station without a license. . . . This is turning it on its head, Your Honor. I know you are inclined, and you've made a determination. But it opens up such hazards to the public interest that I want you to realize what you're doing.

Judge Wilken calmly replied that "I didn't find such egregious hazards on the records. I mean, if there is some further showing that would want to make at some point, I can't prevent you from doing that."

The decision provided Dunifer and his associates with the opportunity to increase the station's power and hours of operation. Within weeks of the decision, the station became a full-fledged twenty-four-hour-a-day, seven-day-a-week operation, broadcasting on 104.1 FM with 30 watts of power from the bathroom studio. "It was pretty loose at that point. People signed up on a chalk board in time slots and we started having meetings," Dunifer said about the bathroom operation. "We later moved into a larger room downstairs [for a studio]. . . . We tried to balance free, democratic open access with some overall vision and mission to what we're doing."

When the station first signed on, volunteers merely wrote their names into a time slot on the chalkboard to sign up for a show. "You didn't have to go through a committee; you didn't have to apply for a slot. You were really encouraged to do a long show, because we didn't have people to fill up the slots," said the Birdman of Berkeley, whose *Resurrection Radio* show mixed political talk and music.[18]

When the time slots were not filled, the station played taped music and political commentaries obtained from Radio Free Maine, David Barsamian's Alternative Radio, and Food Not Bombs. "People from the house used to come into the studio, and if nobody there was doing something, we would turn on the microphone and go crazy," said John Benson, who spent many nights at the station's microphone.[19]

The station attracted an eclectic band of volunteers, including tree-hugging ecologists, punk rock anarchists, street activists, apolitical musicians and wannabes, and Latino and African-American street youths. Chris Thompson, a deejay at the station, concluded that "as the months went by, two separate impulses emerged among the deejays. While Dunifer and the [activists] saw the station as a means to rally the leftist troops and politicize the listeners, the punk rock crowd and others mostly wanted to spin tunes for their friends." The difference in views, lack of organization, and "tensions created by having a radio station where people are living" invariably led to conflicts.

The first conflicts involved residents of the group house and station deejays. "More and more people came into the house who didn't recognize it as a home," said house resident Liquid Jim, who was initially annoyed at having the station in the house, warmed up to the idea, only to get turned off again later. "It was too noisy, there were always people in the house who didn't respect us. . . . We lost a couple roommates because of the strain the station put on us."

Other conflicts erupted that pitted freedom of speech against social responsibility. One was precipitated by deejay Psycho Loco, who hosted a punk rock show filled with "fuck yous," "faggots," and "bitches." When Dunifer, Carol Denney, who cohosted a show with Dunifer, other deejays, and even station listeners asked Psycho Loco to take it easy, he responded with more "fuck yous." As time went on, Psycho Loco became even more belligerent and abusive. After months of fruitlessly trying to convince Psycho Loco to stop, several deejays, Denney, and even Dunifer, an avowed anarchist, believed it was time to establish rules. Some punk rockers confuse "self-centered, nihilistic narcissism with anarchy," said Dunifer about the proposal to establish rules, "but freedom comes with certain responsibility."

A committee was formed that drafted a mission statement describing Free Radio Berkeley as a "vehicle to bring about social change. Consistent with a vision creating an alternative, diverse, hybrid society free of sexism, homophobia, and racism . . . programming on Free Radio Berkeley will be reflective of those goals and ideals."[20] Despite the new mission statement and additional requests that he stop "talking shit," Psycho Loco continued babbling abusively. Finally, the radio collective pulled the plug on his show, causing a number of Psycho Loco's street punk friends to deride the station for being run by "old hippies."

Psycho Loco was not the only programmer whose show produced conflicts among the staff. Chris Thompson, in an article in the alternative weekly, the *Express*, wrote:

> For all its heart-rending trauma, the Psycho Loco controversy was a cakewalk compared with the long, hot summer of 1996. Three back men with dreams of hitting the comedy circuit came across Free Radio Berkeley and found it a perfect vehicle to test their routines and have a couple yucks. They got themselves the Tuesday morning slot and called themselves *Heaven & Hell*, a low-brow trio of John Truhillo, Bishop and Captain Forty-Ouncer. *Heaven & Hell* did schtick, like commercials for the "United Forty-Ouncer Fund"—a forty-ouncer, of course, being a terrible think to waste. They had live reports from Washington, DC, where the "Million Pimp March" was underway. It was truly stirring, said *Heaven & Hell*, to see all the pimps of the world coming together, singing their own version of "We Shall Overcome" entitled "We Shall Slap the Hos."

Carol Denney tuned into the station one morning, hoping to catch the *Earth First!* show. She flicked on her radio fifteen minutes early and caught the tail end of *Heaven & Hell*. The fellas were in the midst of their "Product Tap," in which they called random customer service numbers and asked suggestive questions of the female receptionists. Truhillo claims that they always set up the arrangements with the receptionist off the air first (a pretty weak excuse, if you ask me), but Denney was appalled at what she heard. She called the station and wanted to know just what they thought they were doing.

"A lot of times, people get jacked up on the air and think they're shock jocks," says Denney. "The problem I had was that they were making fun of the women on the air in really derogatory terms. I called the show and asked—very respectfully—if they had ever read the mission statement and if I could talk with them after the show." Truhillo remembers it a little differently. "She called in and cussed us out, attacking us when we had never even heard of her before. She said we shouldn't be saying that stuff on the air, and I tried to say we were just playing comedy roles." Tragically, both are probably right. The content of the *Heaven & Hell* show often provoked an inflamed response in listeners, and the gulf between *lumpen* black culture and middle-class white sensibilities triggered a series of disastrous miscommunications. *Heaven & Hell* and Denney supporters grew increasingly antagonized as the weeks went by . . . , nearly tearing the collective apart. It was white feminism versus the black underclass, a monstrous choice most people dread having to face, but the station had to make it.[21]

According to Thompson, both sides "dug their heels in the dirt." *Heaven & Hell* declared that hip-hop folks don't "follow nobody's rules." In response, Denney informed *Heaven & Hell* that she would be monitoring its next show in a process known as an *air check*. After that, she would decide whether or not to begin proceedings to kick them out of the collective.

The trio responded with a profane, on-air attack against Denney, culminating with a routine on "the joys of necrophilic fellatio." Needless to say, Denney wanted them off the air immediately and called for a meeting of the collective, which had become a nearly all-male club after it failed to take immediate action against Psycho Loco.

When the collective did meet, only two of the twenty-two members who showed up were women. The assembled men were not prepared to take action; instead, they mumbled about revolutionary theory. According to Thompson, "the white men all looked like they were at a tennis game, as their heads swiveled back [and] forth" between *Heaven & Hell* and Denney supporters: "The shades of gray were killing them. At one point the crowd turned to Dunifer, hoping that his radio vision and technical skills could translate into the wisdom that would save the day. But Dunifer's a techie at heart, and when he finally spoke, he muttered something into his beard."

When the vote finally came, the collective failed to resolve the crisis, deadlocking ten to ten. The heated discussion and the failure to resolve the situation led residents of the house where the station was located to fear that the conflict could spill into their home. The residents acted quickly, banning *Heaven & Hell* from the premises, effectively knocking them off the air, and telling Dunifer that Free Radio Berkeley would have to leave.[22]

Dunifer moved the station to an office near North Berkeley's "gourmet ghetto," just a croissant's throw from Chez Panisse and other upscale restaurants. The station broadcast from there between July 1996 and March 1997, when it moved to a larger space in a low-income neighborhood, where it could be closer to its roots among the voiceless.

As Free Radio Berkeley was resolving its staff, location, and programming problems, the situation at KPFA exploded. Long-time programmers like Bill Mandel, who had been a KPFA volunteer for thirty years, were yanked off the air. "I was dumped," said Mandel, who was quietly dropped as a commentator on the morning show in April 1995 "for talking about affirmative action when I was supposed to talk about the Soviet Union. . . . For over a month thereafter, the morning show would go on, but no one ever explained why I wasn't on." A few months later in August Mandel was also removed from his evening show for refusing "to recognize the [station's] gag rule that one must not discuss internal station matters on the air. The new tight-ass control freaks—that's all they can be called—wanted to stop me."[23]

After being dropped by KPFA, Mandel was called by Dunifer, who asked him to join the Free Radio Berkeley staff, and Mandel accepted. Mandel was also recruited as a commentator by KFJC, a station that broadcasts from Foothill Junior College in the South Bay.

Mandel wasn't the only KPFA programmer removed during 1995 and 1996. About sixty programs were eliminated in an effort to air more network-produced programming. According to Mandel, "In the last two years, at every Pacifica station, there has been a reduction of locally-produced programming that has been replaced with nationally-produced programming." The nationally-produced programs include such mainstream material as a talk show featuring former California Governor Jerry Brown, who was elected mayor of Oakland in 1998.

In August KPFA also cancelled Sue Supriano's show, *Steppin' Out of Babylon,* and *Freedom is a Constant Struggle,* a talk and interview show where Kiilu Nyasha was a cohost. As with Bill Mandel, KPFA management was both underhanded and heavy-handed in the way they terminated these shows. "The way they did it was just awful," said Nyasha, an African-American activist who is also disabled. "I was invited to participate in the discussions about the station—actually solicited to be a part—and was never given a clue that 'Freedom' was being cancelled. I felt used and somewhat abused."[24]

Freedom Is a Constant Struggle was not off the air for long, however. Richard Edmondson of San Francisco Liberation Radio invited Nyasha to join that station, and then Dunifer asked her to do a two-hour show on Free Radio Berkeley. Dunifer also asked Supriano to join Free Radio Berkeley, which she did. "There are quite a few former KPFA programmers at Free Radio Berkeley," said Nyasha.

Freedom Is a Constant Struggle is an interview show, where such guests as Ramona Africa, the only adult member of MOVE to survive the 1985 police assault and firebombing of their headquarters in Philadelphia, field Nyasha's and listeners' questions. The show is taped and rebroadcast over San Francisco Liberation Radio later in the week. Nyasha said that she was "surprised to learn" that many nationally-known activists are willing to be interviewed on the unlicensed station.

Supriano also does an interview show, which is taped for rebroadcast on Radio for Peace International, an English-language shortwave station transmitting from Costa Rica. The shortwave station carries many well-known syndicated radio shows, including *RadioNation,* Fairness and Accuracy in Reporting's *CounterSpin,* and David Barsamian's *Alternative Radio.*[25] The influx of former KPFA programmers to Free Radio Berkeley has given the free station a level of professionalism that it lacked before. For example, programmers are now required to be at the station during their assigned times, a big change from the days when the station was located in the group house in North Oakland. "Programmers who miss 2 or more show[s] consecutively without making arrangements for a sub . . . will have to give up that time slot," the collective's statement of "Responsibilities of Programmers" reads. Programmers can also be dismissed for two or more violations of station policy, which prohibits smoking and drinking alcoholic beverages in the studio, stealing CDs or equipment, violence, and violations of the mission statement.

Less disciplined programmers at Free Radio Berkeley immediately complained when the responsibilities statement was adopted. To curb the complaints, Dunifer drafted a curt notice informing programmers that the "lease specifically prohibits smoking, loitering, sleeping and drinking of alcoholic beverages. . . . What we are expecting from every member of this operation is just plain reasonable and responsible behavior. This, in the opinion of some, may be unreasonable or just asking too much. Be that as it may, this is the way it has to be."[26]

The collective also developed application procedures for programmers. Applicants must submit a written proposal for the proposed show to the collective, meet with the scheduling committee, and agree to abide by the mission statement and station policies. The scheduling committee selects among competing applicants using three guidelines: whether the show increases the gender, ethnic, and cultural diversity of the station; the appropriateness of the program for the time slot; and the similarity of the proposed show to those already on. Applicants with little or no radio experience are sent to Flea Radio Berkeley, a low-power portable station that periodically broadcasts on 87.9 MHz on weekends at the Ashby Flea Market. The station is used to promote Free Radio Berkeley and demonstrate how easy it is to put a radio station on the air. "We can go two or three miles with it," Dunifer pointed out.

Free Radio Berkeley has also expanded the type of programming that it offers since moving from the old pink house. On Saturday mornings, the station features *Kidsoundz,* a children's program that offers an alternative to violence-satu-rated television programs. On Saturday evenings, Free Radio Berkeley airs *The Art of Parenting,* a discussion show on child-rearing. "We're the only radio station in the country that I know of that has a parenting show," claimed Dunifer.

The station also carries many of the programs that it started airing when it went to twenty-four-hours-a-day. *Copwatch,* a show that monitors police activi-ties and brutality; the *Radical News Hour,* which carries "news not heard else-where"; and *Acting Globally & Revolting Locally,* an activist show hosted by Steve Dunifer and Laura Drawbridge, have been on Free Radio Berkeley's broadcast schedule for several years. The station continues to play the wide variety of music for which it is best known. On Saturday nights, *Off the Hook & Out of Control* and *Hip Hop Slam* play hip hop. On other nights, listeners can tune in new music, reg-gae, and '60s sounds on *Music Without Boundaries, Cap'n Fred, Spydon,* and *Dead Head Radio.*

The FCC's Order

Nine months after Judge Wilken refused to issue a preliminary injunction stop-ping Free Radio Berkeley from broadcasting, the FCC issued its decision on Dunifer's appeal. As expected, the FCC rejected it. "Dunifer's argument that the Commission's rules abridge an asserted First Amendment right of free speech. Mr. Dunifer's constitutional arguments directly challenge the 60-plus-year statu-tory approach to licensing broadcast transmissions," the decision reported, failing to mention that for sixty years the FCC had defined "public interest" as synony-mous with commercial broadcasting.[27]

The FCC decision contained a large number of misleading assertions. For ex-ample, the FCC suggested that it might have issued Dunifer a license had he ap-plied for one, claiming that "if Mr. Dunifer believes it would be unconstitutional for the FCC to deny him a license, he should have . . . asked for a license, along with a request for a waiver of the relevant rules limiting low power FM service." However, the FCC's suggestion that it might have waived the ban on low-power station operation had the commission's procedures been followed is a lie, accord-ing to John Reed of the FCC's engineering and technology department in Washington, D.C. "I've never heard of [the FCC] giving permission like that," Kane said. "There's never been a case of our approving this."[28]

To bolster its claim that it is willing to license low-power stations, the FCC wrote, "Contrary to Mr. Dunifer's argument, the Commission's rules do not pro-hibit all low power services. For example, the Commission's rules provide for FM translator stations and booster stations which transmit at power well below the 100 watt minimum."[29] In this discussion, the FCC failed to mention that transla-tor and booster stations merely retransmit the signals of already-licensed, large-power stations—and that nearly all translator and booster frequencies have been assigned to corporate broadcasters.

The decision also demonstrated that the FCC was willing to twist logic, in addition to facts, in order to legitimize its policies. When the Commission again mentioned translators, it noted that it had once considered allowing translator stations to originate programming but rejected this in order to "promote program diversity," convolutedly suggesting that fewer, more powerful voices somehow increase diversity. Lastly, the FCC reiterated that it was fining Dunifer more than $1,000, as called for by its rules, because it viewed him as a "recalcitrant individual" who protested "against the regulatory power of the Commission." However, the FCC, hoping to appear benevolent rather than malicious, lowered Dunifer's fine from $20,000 to $10,000, concluding that "$10,000 is an appropriate forfeiture amount."

After issuing its decision and hoping to again avoid a court discussion of the constitutionality of its rules, the FCC filed in federal district court for a "summary judgment" and permanent injunction against Dunifer and Free Radio Berkeley. To win a summary judgment, all the FCC needed to show was that the facts were undisputed (that is, that Free Radio Berkeley was on the air) and that the law was on its side (that is, that Free Radio Berkeley didn't have a license to broadcast).

In its request for summary judgment, the FCC argued that the federal district court has jurisdiction to decide the constitutionality of laws, not rules such as those developed by the FCC, and therefore must not address any of the constitutional issues raised by Dunifer. This argument, however, contradicted what the FCC had asserted a year earlier, when it successfully argued in the U.S. Court of Appeals that the constitutional issues raised by Arizona free radio broadcaster Bill Dougan properly belonged in district court, not the appellate court. The FCC was clearly trying to avoid discussing any constitutional issues, claiming in effect that neither court had jurisdiction. Having filed a friend of the court brief in the Dougan case, Hiken quickly pointed out the FCC's contradictory claims and the appeals court's ruling that district courts can hear challenges to FCC regulations.[30]

The FCC then filed an additional brief asking the court to issue permanent injunctions against the Free Radio Berkeley collective, not just Dunifer, as well as Free Radio Santa Cruz and other stations that the FCC asserted were operated by Dunifer. The commission requested the broad injunction so that it could avoid having to take individual free stations to court, where the constitutionality of its rules could be challenged by each.

The FCC was hoping for a speedy judgment in district court, which it failed to get. Judge Wilken did not issue a preliminary decision until November 1997, which gave the free radio movement time to grow and organize. Between January 1995 and November 1997, hundreds of free radio stations took to the air. Free radio broadcasters also banded together, forming the Association of Micropower Broadcasters, which sponsors conferences, serves as a clearinghouse for technical and legal advice, and provides assistance to stations trying to get off the ground.

Not only did numerous free stations take to the air, but individuals and community groups in large numbers, believing that Judge Wilken's decision legalized free radio broadcasting, contacted the FCC for information on setting up micropower stations. The FCC responded in April 1996—noting that it had received 10,000 inquiries about microradio broadcasting—with a web page called "Low Power Broadcast Radio Stations." Although the web page contains a section written in legalese on "how to start a broadcast radio station," the FCC's attitude toward microradio was easily summarized with the warning, "DON'T DO IT!" The web page warning was accompanied with a statement declaring that unlicensed broadcasters can be fined "a total maximum amount of $75,000" and that unlicensed equipment can "be confiscated."[31]

N O T E S

1. FCC agent Philip Kane told the *East Bay Express* newspaper (August 13, 1993, p. 14) that he received complaints about Free Radio Berkeley from "several" licensed stations, which caused him to monitor and track the station. After the National Lawyers Guild newspaper, the *Conspiracy*, filed a Freedom of Information Act request asking for copies of the complaints, Kane and the agency claimed that the "complaints or inquiries were made in person or by telephone and that no documents or other records were compiled . . . and that the individuals . . . had expressly requested confidentiality." See "Memorandum and Order," *10 FCC Rcd 2155* (January 13, 1995). A separate examination of a complaint about Free Radio Berkeley that the FCC claims to have received from KFOG, a commercial station in San Francisco, "appears to have been prompted by FCC prodding." The FCC received the "complaint" from the station's corporate vice president in New York, who wrote the FCC after hearing about the station at a National Association of Broadcasters (NAB) convention in Las Vegas, where FCC officials spoke. The NAB is the trade association and lobbying group for commercial broadcasters. See Jess Walker, "Don't Touch that Dial," *Reason,* October 1995, p. 32.

2. "Memorandum and Order in the Matter of Application for Review of Stephen Paul Dunifer," NAL/Acct. No. 315SF0050 (released August 2, 1995), on-line posting, available from <http://www.fcc.gov/Bureaus/Miscellaneous/orders/fcc95333.txt>.

3. Stephen Dunifer, in person interview by author, March 4, 1997. Unless otherwise identified, all subsequent remarks by Stephen Dunifer are from this interview.

4. "FCC to Increase Fines for Unlicensed Radio Operations," *67 Radio Register 2nd* (P & F) *619* (March 5, 1990). The FCC had increased its fine for unlicensed broadcasting from $750 to $1,000 in 1990 because of "numerous complaints of interference resulting from 'piracy' of the airwaves." The FCC rationalized the higher fine by asserting that "such malicious practices violate FCC Rules, impede efficient management of the spectrum and frustrate spectrum users."

5. Response to the Notice of Apparent Liability by Louis N. Hiken, addressed to Philip M. Kane, Acting Engineer in Charge, FCC, Hayward, Calif., June 28, 1993.

6. Elaine Herscher, "Do-It-Yourself Radio Broadcasts Over Pirate Station in Berkeley," *San Francisco Chronicle,* June 7, 1993, p. A17.

7. Jeff Cohen and Norman Solomon, "FCC's Highhanded Attack on Low-Watt Broadcaster," *Seattle Times,* December 15, 1994, p. 16; Alexander Cockburn, "Radio Miniwatts Burn the FCC," *Los Angeles Times,* February 2, 1995, p. B7.

8. Kenneth Noble, "FBI's Search for Serial Bomber is Unsettling for Radicals in the Bay Area," *New York Times,* August 8, 1995, p. 19; Joel Achenbach, "The Hunt for Unabomb," *Washington Post,* July 20, 1995, p. C1; and Paul Jacobs, "Unabomber Probe Targets Fringe Groups, Activists," *Los Angeles Times,* July 19, 1995, p. A1.

9. John Batteiger, "Radio Rebels," *San Francisco Bay Guardian,* October 6, 1993, p. 11.

10. Nessie, "Low Wattage, High Influence," *San Francisco Bay Guardian,* February 26, 1997, p. 11.

11. "Defendant's Motion in Opposition to Plaintiff's Motion for Preliminary Injunction," *United States of America v. Stephen Paul Dunifer,* United States District Court, No. C94–03542 CW (December 2, 1994).

12. The Black Hat, "Some Comments and Excerpts from the United States vs. Stephen Dunifer," *Reclaiming the Airwaves,* April/May 1995, p. 3.

13. "Defendant's Motion in Opposition to Plaintiff's Motion for Preliminary Injunction," p. 5.

14. Susan Ferris, "Pirate Roil the Airwaves," *San Francisco Examiner,* January 15, 1995, p. B1.

15. Ricardo Omar Elizalde, "Pirate Radio: Voices of Discontent," *Frontera,* Fall 1996, p. 20.

16. Denis Wagner, "He's Back: Radio Pirate on a Mission," *Phoenix Gazette,* December 19, 1994, p. A1.

17. "Memorandum and Order Denying Plaintiff's Motion for Preliminary Injunction and Staying Action," *United States v. Stephen Paul Dunifer,* United States District Court, No. C 94–03542 CW (January 30, 1995).

18. Chris Thompson, "I Was a Radio Pirate," *East Bay Express,* January 31, 1997, p. 6.

19. Ibid.

20. The mission statement is printed on the instruction sheet, "To All FRB Folks, Please Read — Very Important" (March 1997).

21. Thompson, "I Was a Radio Pirate."

22. Ibid.

23. Bill Mandel, telephone interview by author, June 16, 1997.

24. Kiilu Nyasha, telephone interview by author, June 18, 1997. Unless otherwise identified, all subsequent remarks by Kiilu Nyasha are from this interview.

25. Schedule and frequency information for Radio for Peace International is available at <http://www.clark.net/pub/cwilkins/rfpi/rfpi.html>.

26. "To All FRB Folks, Please Read—Very Important" March 1997.

27. "Memorandum Opinion and Order," in the "Matter of Application for Review of Stephen Paul Dunifer," NAL/Acct. No. 315SF0050 (August 2, 1995).

28. John Reed, telephone interview by author, May 1997.

29. "Memorandum Opinion and Order," p. 4.

30. "The History of Free Radio Berkeley's Legal Battle with the FCC," on-line posting, available from: <http://www.surf.com/~graham/microradio.hundt1.html>.

31. FCC Audio Services Decision, "Low Power Broadcast Radio Station" (April 1996), on-line posting, available from: <http://www.fcc.gov/asd/lowpwr.html#PROHIBITED>. This web site was accessed 9,561 times between January 1, 1997 and October 31, 1997, according to the FCC.

8

The Revolution Widens

The rapid growth of the free radio movement between 1995 and 1997 is due to several factors besides Judge Wilken's decision. Contributing to the growth is the domination of pop music by a few multinational corporations, the development and availability of low-cost FM transmitters, and widespread internet use among free radio broadcasters, which allows for rapid, low-cost information sharing.

In part, the microradio revolution is a revolt against six multinational corporations—Time Warner, Sony (which owns Columbia), Philips Electronics, Seagrams (which owns MCA), Bertelsmann (which owns Arista Records) and EMI—that control 80 percent of pop music sales.[1] Hoping to produce million-selling recordings, these conglomerates sign and promote super groups rather than seeking out cutting-edge artists, and the artists that they do promote tend to be imitations of each other.[2] "The short-sighted, slash-and-burn policies [of the conglomerates] have virtually eradicated any kind of sound, coherent approach to the development of new talent," wrote Michael Greene about this in *Billboard*, the trade magazine of the music industry.[3]

The conglomerates not only control 80 percent of sales, but almost all of the airplay on commercial radio stations, which, like the recording companies, prefer established, "safe" artists like the Rolling Stones to cutting-edge groups. The recording conglomerates also dominate the videos shown on Viacom's MTV.

Because small, independent recording companies, or *indies*, that sign and record promising new musicians have a difficult time getting airplay on commercial radio stations and MTV, they seek out and support new avenues for exposing their artists' recordings. One such avenue is the Worldwide Web, which allows indies to showcase their artists and sell records at the same time. Another is free radio stations, which willingly play the music shunned by corporate-owned stations.

Free radio stations such as Tampa's 87X and Milwaukee's WTPS receive complimentary CDs from indies and, in turn, produce alternative playlists, which are posted in independently-owned record stores. 87X's playlist is dominated by artists on labels such as Moocow, Dischord, and Moon Ska. The independent record stores are also plugged by some free stations, creating a neighborhood-based culture free from corporate dominance.

Even some independent-minded recording artists on corporate labels have used free radio. Pearl Jam, which records on the Sony-owned Epic label, supports Monkey Wrench Radio, a mobile transmitter that broadcasts Pearl Jam concerts from a van accompanying the band on tours. Attendees at Pearl Jam concerts are encouraged to tune to the station before and after the show, and fans who were unable to get or afford concert tickets can still hear Pearl Jam concerts over the microradio station.[4] Ice Cube, who records on Priority Records, which is 50 percent owned by EMI, premiered selections from his *Predator* album on a micropower radio station in South Central Los Angeles.[5] The rapper turned to microradio because he feared that the album would get only limited commercial play because of its controversial lyrics, which included an anti-police rap stating that the Rodney King beating "made me want to go out and pop me a cop."

The production of low-cost FM transmitters and transmitter kits has also fueled the microradio revolution. Stephen Dunifer of Free Radio Berkeley, Doug Brewer, founder of Temple Terrace Community Radio in Florida, and Ernest Wilson, who operates Pan-Com International, produce and sell microradio transmitters for under $150. The three operate web sites describing the equipment that can be accessed from anywhere in the world.

Dunifer's site (www.frb.org) has received over 1,000 inquiries, many from outside the United States, and he has shipped transmitters to Guatemala, Mexico, and Haiti, helping internationalize the microradio revolution. Brewer (www.ld-brewer.com) has also produced and sold many transmitters. Like Dunifer, Brewer has shipped transmitters to countries abroad, including Israel, Chile, and the Philippines. Wilson (www.panaxis.com), the first and for a long time the only U.S. source for FM transmitter kits, has also shipped transmitters abroad, to Argentina, for example, where several thousand micropower stations are on the air.

Not only can micropower transmitters be purchased via the web, but legal information and even station program schedules and playlists can be accessed there. The Committee on Democratic Communications (CDC), which defended Dunifer against the FCC in federal court, has placed its legal briefs on the web (www.surf.com/~graham/microradio.hundtl.html), allowing other microradio broadcasters and their attorneys access to them. This has made it easier for micropower broadcasters to defend themselves against the FCC. The Free Radio Berkeley web site (www.frb.org) provides access to the CDC web site, but also provides programming information to listeners. However, Free Radio Berkeley isn't the only microradio station operating a web site. Radio Mutiny, Lake County Radio in California, Columbia River Radio in Oregon, and numerous other free radio stations have their own web sites.

Also available on the Worldwide Web are sites where free radio broadcasters can obtain programming. Roger Meisner's Radio Free Maine operates a web site (www.cyborganic.com/people/stefan/RadioFreeMaine.html) where micropower and community radio stations can locate alternative programming, such as speeches and interviews with writers like Noam Chomsky, Barbara Ehrenreich, and Howard Zinn, and activists Ralph Nader and Russell Means. Meisner is not the only source of programming available for free radio stations. Bay Area hip-hop deejay Billy Jam syndicates tapes of local hip-hop artists and political commentary, which are distributed as *Pirate Fuckin' Radio* (Box 5124, Berkeley, CA 94705), and Food Not Bombs produces and distributes tapes via the Food Not Bombs Radio Network (3145 Geary Blvd. #12, San Francisco, CA 94118).

The availability of transmitters and syndicated programming made it possible for hundreds of micropower stations to take to the air within a couple of years after Judge Wilken's 1995 decision. In Milwaukee, five new free radio stations appeared during 1996 and 1997, using such call letters as WPRT, BOB-FM, and 88.5 FM. Like the long-established WTPS, WPRT broadcasts to the Bay View neighborhood of Milwaukee and occasionally plugs Rush-Mor Records, an independent record store where WPRT promotional literature can be found. The promotional literature announces that WPRT "is on every night at eight o'clock PM. Tune in boys and girls because your hosts, Captain Jack and Nikita, just might call you to talk live on the air!"[6] BOB-FM broadcasts music and talk to the Riverwest neighborhood, a low-income area of Milwaukee, and 88.5 FM broadcasts on the south end of Bay View, a working class area. The free station on 88.5 FM "has no deejays, no make believe call letters or anything like that," said J. W. Towcar, a former WTPS deejay who operates the station from his home and invites his neighbors to tune in. "The people in the neighborhood know it's on."

Numerous micropower stations have also taken to the air in California and Florida. Northern California has Free Arcata Radio, KBAD (Humboldt), and KBUD (Redwood Valley); central California has Free Radio Fresno, Qwest Radio (Bakersfield), and Pirate Island Radio (Kings River); southern California has Radio Clandestina (Los Angeles), Radio Free San Diego, and Private Radio (Santa Barbara); and the South Bay area has Radio Free San Jose, Free Radio Santa Cruz, and Radio Watson (Watsonville). There are almost as many stations in Florida. To name a few, Ft. Lauderdale has the Bomb and Flavor Radio; Fort Pierce has 106.1 FM; the Tampa-St. Petersburg area has WSAI and La Voz de Ybor; West Palm Beach has MX96; Miami has WEAM, WOMB, Base 9-1-9, and about nine other Spanish language stations; Orlando has Dogg Pound Radio; and Jacksonville has WVOL.[7]

Micropower stations have taken to the air in almost every other major city and region of the United States. In the south, there are Radio Free Memphis, Free Radio The Bayou (Louisiana), and KIND Radio (San Marcos, Texas). In the northeast, there is Steal This Radio (New York City), Radio Mutiny (Philadelphia), and JAM-FM (Syracuse). In the northwest, there are Seattle Liberation Radio, Radio Free Portland, and Radio Free Eugene. In the Ohio valley region, there are Free Radio Pittsburgh, Free Radio Indianapolis, and Free Radio 1055 (Cincinnati). In the Midwest, there are KAW-FM (Lawrence, Kansas), Iowa

City Free Radio, and KCMG-FM (Kansas City). Anchorage, Alaska has three free stations: Glacier City Radio, K-Buzz, and Free Radio Spenard. In each instance, the stations provide services that are not available from commercial radio stations.

For example, Free Radio Memphis (94.7 FM) has a labor show called *Solidarity Forever,* hosted by a member of the Industrial Workers of the World. Guests on the show discuss the difficulties and needs of the labor movement. "They're not getting on there and expressing something they think someone's going to want to buy. They're getting on there and expressing things that are very important to them in an everyday sort of way," said the show's host, comparing his guests with those appearing on commercial stations.[8]

Radio Free Memphis also has a feminist show, *Grrrl Power Hour,"* an indie hip-hop show, and a community news program that covers stories ignored by commercial media. For example, the station aired interviews with activists attending a peace demonstration at the Defense Depot when other media ignored the event.

KAW-FM in Lawrence, Kansas, provides a mixture of indie music programs, talk shows on political and social issues such as economic democracy and campaign finance reform, and forums for neighborhood associations and community groups. "I think it's a good idea to have a station where absolutely anybody can come on who wants or needs airtime," said Ruth Lichtwardt, president of the local Kansas chapter of the League of Women Voters. Not only has KAW-FM received the support of community groups like the League, but the University of Kansas Student Senate passed a resolution supporting the station after the FCC sent KAW a letter ordering it to leave the air.[9]

Other free radio stations also provide services not available elsewhere. Philadelphia's Radio Mutiny has a safe sex call-in show hosted by the Condom Lady; Radio Clandestina has a talk show on politics, sexuality, and health for women of color; Radio Free San Jose has a show for homeless persons; and Steal This Radio features an open mike, providing community members with direct access to the airwaves. Steal This Radio's open mike policy was described by the *New York Times,* which reported that between "9 and 10 P.M. on a recent Friday, a cab driver stopped by to share stories of fares, a guitarist played a song about a friend who worked in a peep show, a social worker talked about vaccinating the homeless, a musician performed finger-style jazz guitar, a disk jockey played records by local bands performing that night and an American Indian recited a family prayer while playing percussion."[10]

Navigating the Stormy Airwaves

Despite many successes, free radio stations have also experienced a number of problems arising from ideological and cultural differences among station personnel, lack of organization, and the difficulties of finding and keeping inexpensive, accessible studio space. The problems encountered by Free Radio Santa Cruz, Free

Radio Fresno, and Radio Illegal typify the problems encountered by many beginning free stations.

Free Radio Santa Cruz was the brainchild of Tom Schreiner, who met Stephen Dunifer while doing graduate work at the University of California at Berkeley and was attracted to micropower radio because of its potential as a community organizing tool. Schreiner encouraged groups in Central California, Mexico, and Guatemala, as well as Santa Cruz, to start microradio stations, and he helped them acquire transmitters for their stations. "While I've helped stations get on the air, I've never operated one myself," said Schreiner, who sees his role as informing others about the potential power of microradio.[11]

"The first station that I helped get on the air was in Santa Cruz," said Schreiner, whose advocacy eventually resulted in the founding of Free Radio Santa Cruz many months after he first proposed the idea. The station's rocky beginning was indicative of problems it would later on have.

One problem Free Radio Santa Cruz initially confronted was that members of the organizing committee had vastly different political views, which led to different ideas about what the station should be. Libertarian Tom Reveille, the founder of Radio Free Venice who moved to Santa Cruz in 1993, proposed that Free Radio Santa Cruz function as a public access station, providing every citizen with access to the microphone. Others supported a collective approach, where the collective decided what programs the station would air. Supporters of the collective approach also differed amongst themselves; participants with anarchistic views favored an open collective that anyone could join, and another group favored a closed collective that would make the decisions about programming and policy. With a closed collective, individuals needed to apply for membership.

In effect, the debates about Free Radio Santa Cruz's direction paralleled debates had taken place earlier at Free Radio Berkeley. After Free Radio Berkeley started broadcasting from North Oakland, it functioned as a public access station; anyone who wanted to broadcast could sign up on the chalk board and have a program. As more discipline was demanded of members, an open collective was created, which debated and established policies for the station. As programming and scheduling became even more rigorous, a smaller group was given responsibility for developing station policy and making programming decisions.

The Free Radio Santa Cruz organizing committee eventually settled on an open collective structure with decisions made by consensus—meaning that everyone had to agree on the policy. Consensus decision-making, while it initially sounded great, ultimately became "frustrating. The meetings were endless and people didn't want to go to them," said Mike Mechanic, who with Alex Torres and Laura Counts had a music show on Free Radio Santa Cruz called the *Monkey Magnet Radio Show.* "We'd have meetings about taking out the garbage that would last three hours." [12] Activist lawyer Ed Frey, also a member of the Free Radio Santa Cruz collective, put it differently: "Nobody was in charge. Nothing got done."[13]

The station got off to a slow start because of these problems. It started broadcasting on 96.3 MHz FM from a small room in the dilapidated home of street activists "Skidmark Bob" Duran, Vincent Lombardo, and Phil Free, but soon moved, largely because programmers had difficulty gaining access to the house—the same problem faced by Free Radio Berkeley when it was located in a residence.[14] Free Radio Santa Cruz then moved to the basement of the residential-commercial building that housed Frey's law office. The new location allowed programmers to enter and leave without hassles.

While in that location, Free Radio Santa Cruz had its golden days. Frey, Mechanic, and a host of other Santa Cruz activists and musicians had shows. The station tried to reach out to homeless persons, radicals, punks, and middle-class liberals with an array of music shows, call-in talk shows, a *Revolution Hour,* and programs about homelessness, such as *Bathrobespierre's Broadsides.*

However, the studio soon turned into a hangout where people "were getting drunk and partying all night," according to Frey. "The radio operators were being very irresponsible." One of the building's residents was recovering from a stroke and could not sleep because of the noise, but there wasn't anything the collective could do about the problems because it was unable to arrive at a consensus about what was unacceptable behavior. The failure to act resulted in the station's being evicted from the building.

The station returned to the small room in the dilapidated house where it began, and many programmers did not want to go there to do shows. The house "was completely run down. It was ready to be condemned. I did one show there," said Mechanic. "I didn't like doing a show in the space. I didn't feel like there was free access and the place was full of garbage. Ultimately, the city inspectors came by and shut them down."

After the house was condemned, Duran, Lombardo, and other residents were told to leave the premises, but rather than leaving, they barricaded themselves in the house. This led to a confrontation with police that split the remnants of the Free Radio Santa Cruz collective. Skidmark Bob, Phil Free, and their supporters depicted the confrontation as an attempt to protect free speech; others viewed it as an unnecessary confrontation.[15]

Regardless of how they interpreted the confrontation, most Free Radio Santa Cruz activists agree that it was the station's last stand. "The station sort of evaporated. They lost their transmitter cite and that was it," said Robert Norse, host of *Bathrobespierre's Broadsides.*[16]

Free Radio Santa Cruz still broadcasts, but only intermittently. "I do a show," said Norse. "You give [Skidmark Bob or Phil Free] tapes" and they air the tapes when they can. However, the station appears to have few listeners. Even people formerly associated with the station—Schreiner, Frey, and others—do not know when, or even if, the station is on the air. The problem with Free Radio Santa Cruz, said Stephen Dunifer, is that "they isolated themselves in the community." To succeed, a free radio station must be part of the community.

The open collective structure proved to be a problem for other free radio stations, including Free Radio Fresno, which inaugurated broadcasting on June 8, 1996, on 105.2 MHz. Anyone could join and go on the air, said Free Radio Fresno's Audrey Alorro. "It was chaos. . . . We just threw it open and said, 'whoever wants to be on the air, go for it.' We want to be twenty-four [hours] and seven [days]," Alorro recalled. "It just degenerated real fast. People wouldn't show up. People just brought their friends in to party on the air. That's no way to run a station. We learned that real fast."[17]

Because of the problems, Radio Free Fresno temporarily went off the air during the first months of 1997, reorganized, and then re-emerged in May on 102.3 MHz. "Now it's a closed collective. You go through an interview. You're asked questions about your politics, your commitment. You have to go through training and you're required to air public service announcements. It's a little more serious now," said Alorro.

The most important requirement for collective members is that they be involved with their communities. "You have to be politically involved in your community first, before you get on the radio, and you have to do something with your politics on the air." Despite the latter requirement, Free Radio Fresno is not filled with boring talk shows or long-winded political harangues. "We still have quite a range of music. There's still a reggae show, some teenagers do a punk, alternative [music] show . . . and we have a world music show. We have quite a mixture," said Alorro.

The closed collective structure has allowed the station to operate smoothly, but it is no longer on twenty-four hours a day. Instead, it broadcasts from 5:00 p.m. to midnight, when most people are off of work. Moreover, the requirement that programmers be politically active in their communities has helped the station become part of the community, which is essential for successful station operation.

An open collective structure and consensus decisionmaking are not the only organizational problems that have dogged free stations, as events at Radio Illegal show. In February 1996, an undocumented U.S. resident from Mexico started Radio Illegal, a Spanish-language station that was operated by a closed collective whose members assumed on-air names such as La Pirans, El Nagual, Mascarita, and "the girl upstairs."[18] The on-air names and even the station's name created an image of mystery and excitement for the station, generating more interest in who the programmers were than in the programming—a problem Radio Free Detroit also created for itself.

In April, three months after Radio Illegal signed on, a reporter from a Bay Area Spanish-language television station, KSTS, visited the station and interviewed several programmers. The three-night television report about the station that finally aired was sensationalistic, emphasizing the station's "illegal operation" and its need to elude the FCC. The reports built on the mystique that the station had created for itself.

The television report, rather than the microradio station's broadcasts, attracted the attention of the FCC, whose agents visited the station on April 26. When they arrived, the agents asked to see the transmitter but were turned away, since they did not have a search warrant. The agents threatened to return the next day with cops and a warrant.

That night, members of the Radio Illegal collective, fearing that the FCC would seize their equipment, disassembled the station and put it into storage. The station's founder also feared that an FCC bust could lead to his deportation, so the station was mothballed rather than being moved to another location.

While the station was off the air, some members of the collective held fundraisers and tried to build community support for the station. In June the collective regrouped and the station returned to the air on 102.5 MHz, calling itself Radio Califa rather than Radio Illegal. The name change was intended to avoid the first mistake—creating a Robin Hood image for the station—and to avoid waving a red flag in the face of the FCC.

When the station returned to the air, it broadcast from noon to midnight, filling in vacant times with recorded programs like *Kidsoundz* and *Steppin' Out of Babylon* that originated on Free Radio Berkeley. It carried cultural programs, music, and some political talk shows, but unlike Free Radio Berkeley, did not have a clear mission. And unlike Radio Illegal, Radio Califa was not a Spanish language station, so it did not provide the Hispanic community with unique programming. Instead, the station duplicated the efforts of Free Radio Berkeley.

The station's raison d'etre seemed to be that it was fun, according to Paul Griffin, who worked at the station. For a few months, the station operated smoothly, but when the excitement among collective members waned, bickering began. Members of the collective no longer saw it as fun. "It was a drag," said Griffin. A very small incident led to the station's abrupt end. One programmer, upset over another's graffiti, changed the lock on the studio door to keep the other out—without informing other members of the collective. The result was that all members of the collective were locked out. Members met and used the incident as an excuse to disband the collective and silence the station. "My perception is that these folks didn't want to follow through, overcoming the problems we had," said Griffin, who argued against going off the air.

After the collective voted to shut down the station, Griffin corresponded with other free radio broadcasters over the internet about the station's demise. Over the net, Temple Terrace Community Radio founder Doug Brewer speculated that the station lacked a central personality "with good leadership abilities." "Every station needs a manager or director," Brewer wrote. His view is partially shared by Tom Schreiner, who advised that stations "need a stable core [of individuals] who can envision being in the same place, giving the station continuity. Because [the collectives] are small, a lot depends on personalities, who does it." Another microbroadcaster suggested over the internet that the "collective was never formally constituted with any charter, bylaws," or the like, a problem that plagued Free Radio Berkeley in its early days. A charter, bylaws, and mission statement can give direction to the collective and station and, without these, irresolvable conflicts can arise.[19]

The internet discussions about the demise of Radio Califa demonstrated the need for an organization that could serve as a free radio clearinghouse, sharing information and insights on how best to deal with problems. To fill this need, Griffin started the Association of Micropower Broadcasters, based in Berkeley, California. The association is a loosely organized support group for free radio broadcasters that disseminates information about the microradio movement. It also publishes an alternative playlist, listing the songs most-frequently played that month on free radio stations.

The association is not the only organizational tool of the microradio movement. The movement also holds conferences, which have steadily attracted more participants. The first microradio conference, organized by Free Radio Berkeley and held in San Jose during early 1996, attracted 150 participants and representatives of fifteen unlicensed stations and other alternative media. Another conference was held in San Francisco on June 15–16, 1996, and another was held a year later in Carson, California. Both attracted nearly 200 participants, including several microbroadcasters from abroad, where the microradio movement is also growing.

International Developments

During the past few years, the free radio movement has spread to several Central American and Caribbean nations, including Guatemala, El Salvador, Mexico, and Haiti.[20] In most of these countries, micropower stations broadcast along with powerful clandestine stations. The micropower stations provide local and neighborhood news, whereas the clandestine stations provide uncensored national and international news.

Several of the Guatemalan micropower stations were founded with help from Tom Schreiner, whose graduate studies took him to villages in Northern Guatemala. These stations broadcast in remote villages using Free Radio Berkeley-built transmitters. By contrast, the Guatemalan National Revolutionary Unity (URNG) guerrilla army operates *La Voz Popular*, which broadcasts to most of the country twice weekly over shortwave.

Since the 1996 signing of the Socio-Economic and Agrarian Agreement that ended Guatemala's civil war, the URNG has demanded that licenses be given to unlicensed stations, something the government has resisted. "The people's movement, its fight, and its ideals must be known to the entire population now that the armed struggle has ended," argued URNG Commander Pablo Monsanto, contending that "radio has and will be our best medium" for achieving that goal.[21]

The URNG's demands are undoubtedly based on events in neighboring El Salvador, where an agreement to end the civil war included provisions for legalizing the Farabundo Martí National Liberation Front's clandestine station, *Radio Venceremos,* but left the ruling Salvadoran oligarchy in control of most of the nation's radio stations. As a result of the oligarchy's near-monopoly over radio, many unlicensed radio stations have gone on the air, broadcasting alternative messages to rural villages and poor neighborhoods using low-cost transmitters, some built by U.S. microbroadcasters. A number of the Salvadoran free stations, like the 20-watt Radio Victoria, operate with micropower. Others, like *Radio Segundo Montes,* which broadcasts from the mountains of Morazán using a 300-watt transmitter, operate with much larger power.[22]

As in the United States, the owners of licensed radio stations and their trade association, the Salvadoran Association of Broadcasters, urged the National Telecommunications Association (ANTEL), El Salvador's FCC, to shut down the unlicensed stations. Responding to this pressure, ANTEL closed and fined eleven micropower stations in December 1995, alleging that their signals interfered with licensed transmissions. A month later, the Salvadoran Supreme Court concluded to the contrary, ruling that ANTEL had improperly silenced the stations. The court overturned ANTEL's fines and ordered the transmitters returned, but also stated that the stations must apply for and get licenses, which is almost as difficult in El Salvador as it is in the United States. As a consequence, ten of the eleven stations resumed broadcasting without licenses and instead petitioned the legislature to grant special status to community radio stations. The oligarchy-controlled legislature rejected the request for special status, but the free radio stations have defiantly remained on the air.[23]

A similar situation exists in Mexico, where the Zapatista National Liberation Army and other guerrillas operate clandestine transmitters from their jungle bases, and civil organizations that support the guerrillas operate unlicensed microradio stations in remote villages. To locate and silence these stations, the government installed twenty-four radio monitoring facilities around the country, with two or more stations installed in the states of Chiapas, Veracruz, and Tamaulipas.[24]

Following the 1991 coup against democratically-elected president Jean-Bertrand Aristide, free radio stations also began broadcasting to Haiti. Although they operated sporadically during the period of military rule, the stations were far more important in organizing a pro-democracy movement than were newspapers, leaflets, or other media because nearly 85 percent of Haiti's population is illiterate.

Immediately following the coup, a powerful clandestine station called *Lavalas Resistence Radio,* named for Aristide's party, went on the air, calling on Aristide supporters to participate in a general strike.[25] Another powerful free station started broadcasting to Haiti in 1994, criticizing the Haitian military regime and the United States, which it said was not doing enough to return Aristide to power. Radio Sunrise (*Radio Soley Leve* in Creole) broadcast on 94.4 MHz and called itself the "vanguard radio of the people's movement for the total and complete liberation of Haiti."[26] The station's anti-U.S. stance apparently motivated the U.S. government to assist Aristide in setting up another clandestine station, Radio Democracy, which broadcast to Haiti from a pro-U.S. perspective for an hour and a half daily.[27] The three stations apparently broadcast from the Dominican Republic.

These clandestine stations were major tools in circumventing Haitian military censorship and demonstrated to Aristide the importance of radio in building a political movement. After he returned to power, Aristide supported the establishment of locally-operated, low-power FM stations.

The purpose of the low-power radio stations is to empower community groups and to serve as a deterrent to further coups or attacks by the paramilitary Tontons Macoutes.[28] Among the stations that took to the air after Aristide's return to power is *Radyo Timoun* (or "Children's Radio"), which directs its broadcasts to Haitians under fifteen, who comprise 40 percent of the population. The station is operated by older children living at the Lafami Selavi orphanage, founded by Aristide in 1986. Radyo Timoun calls itself the "voice of Haiti's future." Like several other Haitian microradio stations, its transmitter came from Free Radio Berkeley.[29]

The microradio revolution has also spread to South America, particularly Brazil and Argentina, where there are more unlicensed microradio stations on the air than in the United States. In the early 1990s, there were just few hundred free stations on the air in Argentina; by the mid-1990s, there were over 3,000.[30]

The Argentinean stations broadcast from shanty towns and poor rural areas to populations neglected by that country's commercial media. Some, like *Justicialist Radio,* are operated by opposition political parties.[31] Many, like Radio Shanty Beats, are operated by young people who, like their counterparts in Haiti, have become politically aware as a result of operating the stations. For example, the young people operating Radio Shanty Beats criticized American film maker Alan Parker for spending most of his time with Argentina's wealthy when researching and filming *Evita.* "Parker insists . . . that the spirit of the story is there, but when it came to the shanty towns, he didn't dare come to us," the station's operator observed.[32]

The Argentinean government has repeatedly attempted to silence these stations. As in the United States, stations have been raided and closed, but others soon appear. For example, in May 1994, the National Telecommunications Commission, Argentina's FCC, closed five stations in Chubut—four in Trelew and one in Puerto Madryn. Overall, they shut down nearly 800 free stations, but their numbers have continued to grow.[33]

The free radio revolution has also spread to Israel, Taiwan, and South Africa. In Israel, where operating an unlicensed station is punishable by three years in jail and a fine of 2.5 million new shekels (NIS), there are between fifty and seventy unlicensed, low-power FM stations on the air. The stations operate with impunity, despite demands by the Israeli Broadcasting Authority, which operates

Israel's licensed radio services, to close them down. The unlicensed stations appear immune to a crackdown because of their ties to politicians; some have direct ties to Israeli political parties, others get protection by providing advertising time to candidates for Israel's legislature, the Knesset.[34]

In Taiwan, the free radio movement was started by opponents of the ruling Kuomintang party, who claim that the government broke its promise to issue radio station licenses to opponents of the ruling party. Instead, the critics point out, new licenses were primarily issued to large corporations controlled by Kuomintang leaders, allowing the ruling party to maintain its media monopoly.

The first free radio station, Voice of Taiwan, was started by Hsu Rong-chi, who discovered a loophole in Taiwan's broadcasting law that limited what the government could do to unlicensed radio operators. The government could impose fines and seize broadcasting equipment, but little more. This allowed free radio stations to continue operating even after a government raid—the free stations merely returned to the air using a spare transmitter.[35] Voice of Taiwan, for example, was raided several times, but each time returned to the air within a few hours or days of the raid.[36]

Hsu started broadcasting on November 23, 1993, from a 200-watt transmitter strategically placed in a mountaintop Buddhist temple north of Taipei, which allowed him to reach most of the capital. Hsu's anti-government programs attracted a large, dedicated following. In February 1994, his attacks on high insurance premiums led cabbies to blockade the Finance Ministry. Two months later, several hundred cabbies surrounded an historic building about to be razed after Hsu called for it to be preserved as a historic site.[37] When police attempted to disperse the cabbies, a riot broke out, which gave the government an excuse for arresting Hsu on incitement to riot charges.

Within a year of Voice of Taiwan's inaugural broadcast, nearly forty unlicensed stations, most operated by Kuomintang opponents, were on the air. They include Greenpeace Radio, the New Voice of Formosa, and Voice of the People. Greenpeace Radio carries many environmental programs, but also features live call-in shows, such as *Three Aunts, Six Grandmothers,* a program addressing issues of interest to women. The New Voice of Formosa broadcasts Hakka dialect programs. Like Voice of Taiwan, the operators of the New Voice were arrested for incitement when, during a discussion about police clubbing demonstrators in an anti-government protest, a speaker threatened to use Molotov cocktails against police.

Voice of the People carries programming about government corruption, nepotism, and incompetence. "We appeal to the lower rung of society, taxi drivers and bean curd sellers," said station operator Antonio Li. "We give the unspoken society a voice."[38]

When police raided fourteen free radio stations in September 1994, Voice of the People called for protests, which quickly turned confrontational. As the Reuters news service reported,

Taiwan police Monday battled hundreds of demonstrators who smashed windows of government offices, burned cars and beat up photographers to protest a crackdown on illegal radio stations. Hundreds of helmeted riot police sprayed the protesters with water cannons to try to halt a hail of stones and bricks that shattered most ground floor windows of the Government Information Office.[39]

Not only have Taiwan's free stations rallied citizens around specific issues, but they have changed the political landscape by breaking the Kuomintang's broadcasting monopoly. As *Asiaweek* reported, "Pirate radio shows [have] reduced the appeal of mass rallies and the effectiveness of government-controlled TV stations. Voters are better informed."[40] As a result, the opposition Democratic Progressive Party candidate won Taipei's mayoral election in December 1994. The new mayor promised to stop the police raids and to help unlicensed opposition stations get broadcasting licenses. Democratic Progressive Party spokesperson Chen Fangmin summed up the party's relationship with Taiwan's free radio stations, saying, "It is hard to tell if we could have won without the radio stations."[41]

In South Africa, the government of President Nelson Mandela has promoted community radio, but unlicensed stations continue to operate there. The unlicensed stations are mostly ethnic or tribal stations that attempt to disunite, rather than unite, the nation. Some, like Radio Liberty and Radio Donkerhoek, are operated by Afrikaners, who use the stations to attack Mandela's government.

Unlike the United States, South Africa has been tolerant of the unlicensed stations, even though they have created headaches for the government.[42] One reason for this tolerance is that President Mandela's African National Congress (ANC) for many years operated an unlicensed station called Radio Freedom, which broadcast anti-apartheid programs to South Africa from powerful shortwave transmitters located in Zambia, Tanzania, and Zimbabwe. The station became a symbol of ANC opposition to the white-led South African government and was widely listened to by black South Africans.

After Mandela became president, Radio Freedom moved to Johannesburg and established a media institute called the Audio Waves Foundation that trains young South Africans to become broadcasters. The hope is that the young broadcasters will return to their homes after the training and operate community stations that will program locally, but will also carry national news, thus unifying the nation.[43]

Another reason why the South African government has been tolerant of unlicensed stations is that it has secretly allowed a number of pro-democracy clandestine stations to broadcast against African dictators from its territory. One South African–based clandestine station is Radio Kudirat, which broadcasts to Nigeria from a 500-kilowatt shortwave transmitter. The station broadcasts one hour each night, signing on with the statement: "The time is five minutes past eight. This is Radio Kudirat Nigeria—the voice of democracy."

The station is named for Al-Hajji Kudirat, deposed president Moshood Abiola's wife, who was assassinated shortly after the coup. Wole Solinka, a spokesperson for the National Liberation Council of Nigeria, which operates the station, said that they named it for Kudirat to "send a very clear message to the junta that assassinating or rubbing out or incarcerating individuals can never get rid of the idea that we are trying to push. And there's no better way than to haunt them daily with the name of a woman we suspect them of murdering."[44]

Radio Kudirat Nigeria is not the only pro-democracy station broadcasting to Nigeria. On June 12, 1997, the Free Nigeria Movement, an exile group opposed to Nigeria's military kleptocracy, started the Voice of Free Nigeria. The station broadcasts two hours daily—one hour in the morning and one hour in the evening—on 7180 KHz shortwave. The station "is intended to serve as a source of information, education and entertainment to the Nigerian people."[45] Like Radio Kudirat Nigeria, the transmitter of this station is probably located outside, rather than inside, Nigeria.

There is also a low-power, pro-democracy FM station that broadcasts from a transmitter hidden in Lagos.[46] The station calls itself The Freedom Frequency and appears sporadically to avoid detection. If the station had scheduled hours, as Radio Kudirat Nigeria and the Voice of Free Nigeria do, it could be easily located and silenced by the Nigerian military. But by operating sporadically, the station is difficult for authorities to locate. By the time the army and police have figured out that the station is on the air, it is off again and cannot be located.

The operation of The Freedom Frequency underscores the disadvantages of operating a microradio station under conditions of repression: The station must appear unannounced to avoid being detected and, as a result, is unlikely to generate a large audience. Only listeners who are scanning their receivers when the station is broadcasting are likely to locate and listen to the broadcasts. Moreover, the broadcasts must be kept short, limiting what can be said. The longer that the station is on the air, the greater the likelihood that the station will be located by authorities, making seizure more likely. This explains why powerful shortwave stations, which can blanket large areas by bouncing their signals off the ionosphere, are a better medium than microradio stations for circumventing censorship where governments are repressive, as in Nigeria and Burma.

NOTES

1. "The Media Nation," *Nation,* August 25, 1997, pp. 27–30.

2. Robert Hiburn and Chuck Philips, "What's Wrong with the Record Industry (and How to Fix It)," *Los Angeles Times,* October 12, 1997, p. C5.

3. Michael Greene, "How to Keep the Sky from Falling," *Billboard,* February 15, 1997, p. 16.

4. Chris Becker, "We Don't Need No Stinking License," *Factsheet Five* 59:11.

5. Beth Kleid, "Morning Report," *Los Angeles Times,* November 2, 1992, p. F2.

6. Larry Soley, "Milwaukee Pirates Challenge Narrow Music Formats," *Milwaukee Shepherd Express,* September 18, 1997, p. 11.

7. David D. Porter, "Dogg Pound Radio: Unlicensed, Unique," *Orlando Sentinel Tribune,* December 11, 1997, p. D1; Michael Canning, "Pirates of the Airwaves," *St. Petersburg Times,* July 9, 1997, p. 1D; Terry L. Krueger, *Florida Low Power Stations* (Clearwater, Fla.: Tocobaga Publications, 1996); "Free Radio USA," *Slingshot,* February 1997, p. 4.

8. Jim Hanas, "Free Radio Memphis Remains on the Air," *Memphis Flyer,* November 27, 1997, p. 16.

9. Tom Perrin, "Radio Station Fighting for Airwaves," *Kansas City Star,* November 13, 1997, p. A1.

10. Neil Strauss, "Pirate Radio in Touch With the Village, Not the F.C.C." *New York Times,* February 27, 1996, p. C11.

11. Tom Schreiner, telephone interview by author, July 16, 1997.

12. Mike Mechanic, telephone interview by author, July 24, 1997.

13. Ed Frey, telephone interview by author, March 1, 1997.

14. Michael Mechanic, "A Radio Revolution," *Metro Santa Cruz,* February 1–7, 1996, p. 5.

15. According to newspaper accounts, Duran, Free, Lombardo, and their friends booby-trapped the house with containers of urine, which hit the police when they entered. The protestors claim that police spilled the urine on themselves when removing the containers from the house, but offer several different explanations for why the containers were filled with urine. Ultimately, most leftists in Santa Cruz, including socialist mayor Mike Rotkin and many former Free Radio Santa Cruz activists, denounced the protestors for "being completely out of control." See John Woolfolk, "Santa Cruz's Bad Dream Activists Chide Liberal City on Treatment of Homeless," *San Jose Mercury News,* September 17, 1996, p. 1A; Lee Quarnstrom, "Protesters' Nasty Tactics Outrage Santa Cruz City Leaders," *San Jose Mercury News,* August 26, 1996, p. 1B.

16. Robert Norse, telephone interview by author, March 1, 1997.

17. Audrey Alorro, telephone interview by author, July 28, 1997. Unless otherwise identified, all subsequent remarks by Audrey Alorro are from this interview.

18. Paul W. Griffin, in person interview by author, March 4, 1996.

19. On-line posting, available from: <http://www.frn.net/lpfm-grapevine/>, January 20, 1997.

20. Kenneth Noble, "Is Pirate Radio Guru a Champion of Democracy or Public Menace?" *New York Times,* January 28, 1996, p. A4.

21. British Broadcasting Corporation, "Other Reports: Frequency for Voz Popular Radio is Part of Peace Process," *BBC Summary of World Broadcasts,* May 23, 1996, pp. 0021.

22. Diana Agosta, e-mail to author, December 20, 1997; Cristina Starr, e-mail to author, January 6, 1998.

23. U.S. Department of State, *El Salvador Country Report on Human Rights Practices for 1996* (Human Rights Country Reports), February 1997.

24. Foreign Broadcast Information Service, "Secretariat to Locate 'Clandestine' Radios," *Daily Report,* April 29, 1994.

25. United Press International, "Haiti Tense on Eve of General Strike," October 23, 1991, BC cycle.

26. Foreign Broadcast Information Service, "Clandestine Radio Blames U.S. for Coup d'Etat," *Daily Reports,* April 12, 1994; Foreign Broadcast Information Service, " Haiti," *FBIS Media Guide,* September 16, 1994.

27. Foreign Broadcast Information Service, "Port-au-Prince Signal FM Radio," *Daily Report,* July 18, 1994.

28. The Tontons-Macoutes also operated a clandestine station called VSN–57 following the coup. See "Haitian Parliament Split Over OAS Plan," United Press International, December 17, 1991, BC cycle; Inter Press Service, "Haiti: Press Under Attack Since Aristide's Ouster, Says Report," September 25, 1992.

29. Lyn Duff, "Kids' Radio Gives Voice to Haiti's Future," *San Francisco Examiner,* February 6, 1996, p. B7.

30. Ellen Torres, "Latin TV Industry Meets in Buenos Aires," *Video Age International,* October 1995, p. 38.

31. Foreign Broadcast Information Service, "Daily Report," April 28, 1994.

32. Claude Nye, "The Making of Evita Turned a Country Upside Down," *Guardian,* December 20, 1996, p. T6.

33. Foreign Broadcast Information Service, *Daily Reports,* June 5, 1994; Jesse Walker, "Don't Touch that Dial," *Reason,* October 1995, p. 34.

34. Helen Kaye, "Nahman Shai: Government is Ignoring Law Against Pirate Radio Stations," *Jerusalem Post,* April 18, 1996, p. 12.

35. Susan Yu, "Raid on Pirate Radio Station Shows Government Resolve," *Free China Journal,* January 7, 1995.

36. Joyce Liu, "Host of Pirate Radio Station Whips Up Controversy," Reuters North American Service, October 7, 1994.

37. Steven A. Chin, "Airwave Warrior Takes on Government," *San Francisco Examiner,* February 21, 1995, p. A2.

38. Rone Tempest, "Pirate Radio Captures Taiwanese Politics—And Culture," *Los Angeles Times,* January 3, 1995, p. 3.

39. Alice Hung, "Taiwan Protestors Battle Police Over Radio Station," Reuters North American Wire, August 1, 1994.

40. "Three-Way Rule? December's Elections May Be a Turning Point," *Asiaweek,* December 1, 1995, p. 41.

41. Tempest, "Pirate Radio Captures Taiwanese Politics—and Culture," p. 3.

42. Although the government tries to avoid antagonizing the operators of these stations, the broadcasts of Radio Donkerhoek were so extreme that the South African Broadcasting Corporation tried to close the station down in 1995, but backed off after the operator barricaded himself in the studio and broadcast for help. About 300 white right-wingers responded to the broadcasts and rallied to defend the station. See British Broadcasting Corporation, *Summary of World Broadcast,* April 28, 1995.

43. British Broadcasting Corporation, *Summary of World Broadcasts,* June 14, 1994, p. 2021.

44. British Broadcasting Corporation, *Summary of World Broadcasts,* January 14, 1997. The station managed to keep its location secret for the first months of operation, when it was called Radio Democrat International, but the BBC traced the clandestine station's transmitter to South Africa.

45. "Free Nigeria Movement," June 8, 1997, on-line posting, disussion list, available e-mail: CORPORATIONS@envirolink.org; on-line posting, available from:<http://pw2.net-com.com/~fnm>.

46. British Broadcasting Corporation, *Summary of World Broadcasts,* March 1, 1996.

9

The Counterrevolution

Soon after the first free radio station appeared in 1931, the Czechoslovak government, which was the target of the unlicensed broadcasts, tried to locate and silence the station. Since that time, governments have responded in similar fashion to the appearance of free stations. Governments have attacked and bombed guerrilla transmitters, pressured neighboring states into silencing unlicensed stations broadcasting from their territory, and seized the transmitters of pirate radio stations and fined their operators. Examples of each type of government action are numerous.

During the Salvadoran civil war of the 1980s, a major objective of the government was to silence Radio Venceremos, a guerrilla-operated station that broadcast from Morazán province. Attempts to silence the guerrilla station led to numerous military encounters and deaths, including that of Colonel Domingo Monterrosa. Monterrosa, one of the army's leading commanders, attacked a rebel base where he believed Radio Venceremos was located. There, Monterrosa unknowingly found, not the real transmitter, but a booby-trapped transmitter, which he attempted to transport back to San Salvador by helicopter. The booby-transmitter exploded en route, downing the helicopter and killing Monterrosa.[1]

In Colombia during the early 1990s, the government not only attacked guerrilla camps in an effort to silence the clandestine *Radio Patria Libre,* but tried to bomb the station as well.[2] More recently, the Burmese military attempted to silence an anti-government broadcasting station by invading the remote jungle area where the studio was located. The programmers, mostly members of the All Burma Students Democratic Front, fled across the border into Thailand, where they built another studio.[3]

Governments also use diplomatic pressure to silence free stations when they believe that the unlicensed transmissions are supported by or located in a foreign country. In 1992 Papua New Guinea's foreign ministry delivered a protest note to Australian authorities because Australian technicians helped the Bougainville Revolutionary Army establish Radio Free Bougainville, which demands independence for the island of Bougainville, populated by people who are ethnically distinct from the Papuans. The Papua New Guinea government declared the station to be "an act of espionage and terrorism."[4] The same year, Burundi's ambassador to Rwanda "expressed concerns" to Rwandan Minister of Information Pascal Ndengejeho over an unlicensed station broadcasting to his country from Rwanda. The station attempted to foment distrust between the majority Hutus and the minority Tutsis, who had long dominated Burundi's government and military. The station was part of a simmering distrust between the two ethnic groups that erupted into a civil war and series of massacres in 1994.[5]

The most common action taken by governments is to simply raid unlicensed stations and seize their transmitters, thereby forcing them off the air. This was standard practice in France until the election of Socialist president Francois Mitterrand.

Where laws have restricted the actions that authorities can take to do stop unlicensed broadcasting, governments often change the law, making it easier for them to shut down free stations. This is what occurred in Taiwan. Faced with election defeats and its loss of control over Taiwan's media, the Kuomintang party amended the Telecommunications Act, allowing it to more easily close down free radio stations. Effective February 1996, fines for unlicensed broadcasting were substantially increased and imprisonment was imposed as a punishment. The amendment contained a six-month grace period during which unlicensed stations could apply for licenses, which many did. The telecommunications ministry refused to grant licenses to many stations, claiming that they failed to meet its requirements, but the unlicensed stations remained on the air anyway.[6]

A similar strategy was pursued in the United States by the FCC in an effort to curb the growing number of free stations. Confronted by a court decision that invalidated its forfeiture rules,[7] Judge Claudia Wilken's acceptance of arguments presented in federal district court that the FCC was fining free radio broadcasters more than the amounts set by FCC rules,[8] and lobbying by the National Association of Broadcasters (NAB) to take more decisive action against unlicensed broadcasting stations, the FCC issued new rules in June 1997 that reiterated a fine of $10,000 for the "construction and/or operation without an instrument of authorization for the services."[9]

As with most other FCC inquiries and rulemakings, this one occurred with almost no public input. All but two of the comments filed in the rulemaking were from telecommunication corporations or their trade associations, including the NAB. The comment of the one private citizen who filed—Bill Dougan of Arizona Free Radio—was treated as an informal rather than formal comment by the Commission, and the fine structure that was adopted reflected the interests of the corporations involved in the rulemaking. The $10,000 fine for operating a station without a license was the highest fine set for any rules violation, exceeding the amount levied for committing "fraud by wire, radio or television" ($5,000), broadcasting indecent or obscene materials ($7,000), or violating political rules, such as giving free commercial time to one but not other political candidates ($9,000). The level of fines clearly demonstrates the FCC's thinking—that it is more important to protect commercial broadcasters' control of the electromagnetic spectrum than it is to protect the public from commercial fraud.

FCC-NAB Complicity

Shortly after Judge Wilken refused to issue a preliminary injunction against Free Radio Berkeley in January 1995, the general counsel of the FCC contacted the NAB's policy office, asking whether the NAB believed that there were any legitimate First Amendment issues involved in the Free Radio Berkeley case, as Judge Wilken had concluded. The NAB predictably responded that there were not, so the FCC counsel asked the NAB if it would get involved in the case, filing a brief on behalf of the Commission that explained to Judge Wilken "how deeply wrong" her decision was. The NAB was "very happy to do that," says Jack Goodman, a vice president and attorney for the NAB, pointing out that the Commission's limitations on citizen access to the airwaves are "the absolute bedrock of FCC regulation."[10]

The NAB filed an amicus brief, arguing that "the Supreme Court has rejected the notion of unlicensed operation" and that the District Court cannot rule on the constitutionality of FCC regulations, which was what the FCC argued. Goodman also flew to San Francisco for the oral arguments in the case, where he encountered a demonstration at the federal courthouse in support of Free Radio Berkeley. "It was quite an event," Goodman complained. "There was a huge demonstration in front of the courthouse. Dunifer and his cohorts attempted to pack the courtroom."[11]

After Judge Wilken refused the FCC's request for summary judgment and a permanent injunction against Free Radio Berkeley in 1996, the NAB pledged that it "will continue to support the Commission." As part of this support, NAB representatives met privately with FCC officials, trying to come up with ways to drive free radio stations off the air. As NAB spokesman Jack Goodman put it, "We have been working very closely with the FCC to try and speed up and help their process along. And we continue to have discussions with them about differing ways that can be done. And we are going to continue to work with them to try to nip this sudden spurt of pirate radio in the bud."[12]

Because of the defeats it suffered in Judge Wilken's courtroom, the FCC was reluctant to take direct action against free radio broadcasters, despite complaints from commercial broadcasters and the lobbying by their trade association. Instead the Commission merely issued statements reaffirming its opposition to unlicensed radio operations.[13]

As complaints from commercial broadcasters mounted, the FCC eventually targeted for closing a few unlicensed stations in the South and Midwest—far from Judge Wilken's court. In addition to their geographic locations, the targeted unlicensed stations had two things in common: The stations were operated by individuals without community participation and their programs often differed from that of most microradio broadcasters, which often speak for disenfranchised communities.

The strategy that the FCC pursued in each case was the same. Rather than seeking an injunction against them, as the Commission had done with Free Radio Berkeley, FCC agents, accompanied by law enforcement officials, seized the stations' transmitters. By seizing the transmitters, the FCC immediately put the free radio broadcasters off the air and on the defensive, requiring them to go to court to get their transmitters back, where they would be required to show that they had a legal right to operate the transmitters. Proving this to a court would be very difficult.

The first station the FCC targeted was Lutz Community Radio near Tampa, Florida, operated by Lonnie Kobres. Most of the programming carried by the station was downloaded from satellite feeds rather than originated locally, so that community members had little involvement in producing programs or influencing the station's content.

The FCC had been aware for many months that Kobres's station was on the air, having first monitored its broadcasts on October 31, 1995. After the monitoring, Kobres was sent letters by the FCC, informing him that the broadcasts were illegal. On March 8, 1996—less than a year after the bombing of the Alfred P. Murrah Federal Building in Oklahoma City, which spawned a frenzy of media reports that equated "constitutionalists" like Kobres with the Oklahoma City bombers—federal agents with search warrants raided the Lutz radio station and seized its transmitter. The widespread public antipathy to the far-right movement that resulted from the Oklahoma City bombing and the media's coverage of it made Kobres an easy target, although the FCC denied that Kobres was targeted because of his political views. Kobres's views were "not an issue," said Ralph Barlow, an FCC engineer in charge of the Tampa office.[14] Despite the denial, Kobres's was the only station raided, even though several other unlicensed stations were on the air at the time in the Tampa area. Barlow contended that Kobres's station was raided because of repeated complaints from the commercial broadcasters in the area that the station interfered with their broadcasts.

In June the FCC raided Black Liberation Radio 2 in Richmond, Virginia, which had been on the air for less than six months. The station was operated by Jahi Kubweza and his family rather than a community group and was patterned after the Illinois-based free station, Black Liberation Radio. As with Lutz Community Radio, FCC agents visited Kubweza's home, demanded to see the transmitter, and then seized it.[15]

The FCC used a similar approach to silence The Beat, a pirate station operated by Alan Freed in Minneapolis that carried dance music. The 20-watt station, based in Freed's apartment, signed on July 21, 1996, and soon attracted an audience in Minneapolis's hip Uptown neighborhood. The station also attracted the enmity of commercial broadcasting corporations and the Minnesota Broadcasters Association, which almost immediately filed complaints with the FCC.[16]

In August the FCC responded to the complaints, sending Freed a letter warning him that he could be fined and imprisoned for operating a radio station without a license. Freed responded with a letter challenging the constitutionality of the FCC's rules banning low-power radio stations. He continued broadcasting, despite the warning letter and other harassment, which included anonymous threats and repeated interference on 97.7 FM, the frequency on which the station broadcast.[17] In October, the FCC went before a federal magistrate and asked for an arrest warrant directing the U.S. marshall to seize Freed's transmitter. The court issued the warrant and in November the transmitter was seized.

A month later, on December 11, 1996, FCC agents from Tampa travelled to Orlando, where they investigated a complaint filed by local broadcasters against an unlicensed station broadcasting on 106.5 FM. Like The Beat, the Orlando station broadcast music rather than community affairs programs. As they did in Lutz, Richmond, and Minneapolis, the agents confiscated this station's transmitting equipment, thereby silencing the station.[18]

Kobres and Freed responded to the seizures by filing claims in federal court, requesting that the FCC return their equipment because the seizures were unlawful. Both challenged the constitutionality of FCC rules governing low-power broadcasts in their filings. Lonnie Kobres also acquired another transmitter and put Lutz Community Radio back on the air, something neither Kubweza nor Freed attempted.

These FCC actions were not enough to please the NAB, which urged the FCC to be even more resolute with free radio broadcasters. To underscore its opposition to free radio broadcasting, the NAB scheduled a forum on "pirate radio" at its 1997 annual conference in Las Vegas, to which it invited Beverly Baker, chief of the Compliance and Information Bureau, which has the responsibility for shutting down free stations. Also on the panel were Bill Ruck of KFOG-FM, a commercial station in San Francisco, who claimed that San Francisco Liberation Radio and Free Radio Berkeley were interfering with licensed stations, and NAB Vice President Jack Goodman, who described how the FCC and NAB were working together to get free radio broadcasters off the air.

To the assembled NAB members, Baker described the "tools" available to the FCC for silencing free radio stations. "We will send them a letter" explaining that they are violating the law, Baker said. "The other tools we have to use [include] forfeitures—$11,000 now for each instance. We can also with the help of the U.S. Attorney's office . . . go after the 'stuff.' We can get the 'things.' We can go in and seize the equipment that the unlicensed operator is using. That is my personal favorite," Baker confided. "We can also go for injunctions . . . and in some cases, there are criminal penalties. It's not likely that we would go for a criminal penalty in very many cases," she added.[19]

Baker, however, explained that the FCC felt constrained in using these tools because of Judge Wilken's decision, saying, "The problems that are currently complicating and escalating the unlicensed operator problem are first of all, this U.S. District Court case on a preliminary injunction where the judge denied our preliminary injunction request, suggesting that maybe we ought to look at whether there was a First Amendment issue here. We do not believe there is a First Amendment issue. . . . We think this is nonsense."

More importantly, Baker advised commercial broadcasters on how they could help the FCC in silencing free radio operators. "You can help us by first of all letting us know about the pirates in your area. . . . The more you can tell us about them, the easier it will be for us to deal with them." Baker also suggested that the broadcasters apply economic pressure on unlicensed broadcasters by having music licensing organizations such as BMI (Broadcast Music, Inc.) and ASCAP (American Society of Composers, Authors, and Publishers) seek royalty payments from free radio stations. Finally, in the question-and-answer period, which became a complaint session, Baker promised broadcasters that she would look into unlicensed radio operations in their areas. "If you give me your business card, I'll check up on your problem," she told several broadcasters.[20]

Several broadcasting corporations and local broadcaster organizations responded to Baker's offer. In Wisconsin, the Milwaukee Area Radio Stations (MARS) trade organization filed a complaint with the FCC in late May, asking it to take action against unlicensed stations operating in that city. The complaint listed the unlicensed stations and their locations.[21]

The FCC responded by writing letters to the free stations turned in by MARS. At least one, WGAY, temporarily signed off after receiving the letter. Another, WTPS, Milwaukee's longest-operating free station, also signed off, not just because of the complaints from MARS, but because the station's operator was being harassed by a local crank and because a large broadcasting corporation, Saga Communications, petitioned the FCC to put a translator on 99.9 MHz, the frequency on which WTPS broadcast.[22] Finally, the NAB Radio Board asked the FCC in June to silence even more free radio stations. The NAB demanded that "'pirate' radio broadcast operations are terminated promptly" and operators "are prosecuted to the fullest extent of the law."[23]

It took the U.S. District Courts in Florida and Minnesota about a year to rule on Kobres's and Freed's claims. On August 24, 1997, the court in Florida upheld the government's seizure of the Kobres transmitter.[24] On September 5, 1997, the court in Minnesota also decided in the FCC's favor. The Minnesota court ruled that the U.S. Court of Appeals, not district courts, have jurisdiction over the constitutionality of FCC rules, as the FCC had argued. The Minnesota decision handed the FCC a decision that it had failed to get in Judge Wilken's court and a green light to move against free radio broadcasters in districts outside of the San Francisco Bay Area.

The FCC immediately publicized its victories in press releases and on its website, even though Freed appealed the court decision. The press release and website announced: "FCC Wins Court Action Against Unlicensed Radio Operator."[25]

Freed's appeal was filed in the Eighth Circuit Court of Appeals, where he again argued that the FCC's rules were unconstitutional. Recognizing the threat that the appeal posed to commercial broadcasters, the NAB intervened in the case, filing an amicus brief in support of the FCC. The NAB's brief argued that the court should uphold the district court's ruling, but should not rule on the constitutionality of the FCC ban on low-power broadcasting "because the FCC was enforcing the statutory ban on unlicensed broadcasting, not FCC power regulations." The brief was clearly designed to avoid discussing FCC rules, which favor corporate broadcasters.[26]

The FCC's Offensive

It didn't take long after the district court decisions for the FCC to start an offensive against free radio broadcasters.[27] Within weeks, the FCC was notifying unlicensed stations to close down and dispatching agents to seize the "stuff." The first stations targeted were pirates, but the FCC soon thereafter moved against community-operated microradio stations.

On September 4, 1997, FCC agents and U.S. marshals, acting on a complaint filed by New Jersey Broadcasting, Inc., which owned four commercial stations in New Jersey, raided a pirate station in Howell, New Jersey that called itself Oldies 104.7 FM. This pirate station differed from most free stations in that it carried commercials, promoted itself on billboards, and was a member of the local chamber of commerce. The station's operator, Salvatore DeRogatis, was apparently stunned by the raid. "I thought they would never shut me down because of what had happened in California," said DeRogatis, alluding to Judge Wilken's decision but apparently unaware that the decision applied only to that court district. In response to the raid, the corporate broadcaster who complained to the FCC announced that she was "very pleased at the FCC's swift and immediate action."[28]

Two weeks later, FCC agents, backed by twelve federal marshals and six sheriff's deputies, seized the equipment of Community Power Radio, an unlicensed station that broadcast to African-Americans in the Oak Park neighborhood of Sacramento, California.[29] The FCC raid was in response to complaints filed by several licensed stations, including KVIE-TV, a public television affiliate on Channel 6, which is adjacent to the FM band in the broadcasting spectrum. Community Power Radio had been on and off the air since December 1995, closing down twice after warnings from the FCC, but reappearing again a few weeks later. It was inspired by the 1995 Million Man March in Washington, D.C., which was organized by Louis Farrakhan's Nation of Islam and called on black men to improve their communities and become economically self-sufficient. The station's founder, Abdul Rahman Muhammad, was a member of the Nation of Islam and the station frequently broadcast speeches of Farrakhan.[30] Consistent with Farrakhan's views, the station helped sponsor community events such as meals for low-income residents.

Community Power Radio also carried rhythm and blues, rap, jazz, gospel music, and talk and information programs sponsored by local businesses such as Sam's Cheaper Store, but community groups and individuals also donated to the station. After the FCC raid, Muhammad called a press conference attended by three dozen supporters where he vowed to return to the air, saying, "We will open in Del Paso Heights, in North Highland, in South Sacramento."[31]

In October the FCC also shut down several other stations, including 105.5 FM in Miami, 106.5 FM in West Palm Beach, KCMG-FM in Kansas City, and Radio Free Allston, a high-profile community station in Boston whose visibility was the result of its being organized and operated openly.[32] Free Radio Allston was started by "a diverse team of community activists, anti-censorship advocates and left-leaning political free-thinkers," who attended a meeting in January 1997 at a local school. The meeting was called by Steve Provizer, who believed that the neighborhood needed a station that could function "as a community newspaper of sorts." The first meeting, which was widely publicized, attracted forty people, many of whom helped get the station off the ground.[33]

When it finally took to the airwaves in March, Radio Free Allston broadcast from public locations such as cafes, rather than from an underground studio. In these public locations, the station was able to provide the community with direct access to the airwaves, something no commercial station was doing. In describing the station, Provizer said, "We're completely diverse, anti-format radio. . . . We do the programs people bring, including Brazilian, Creole and Spanish programs."[34] In fact, the station provided far more service to the community than did commercial stations in Boston. For example, it was the only medium that covered a forum of at-large City Council candidates held in Brighton.[35] Such coverage prompted the City Council to pass a resolution backing non-profit status for the station, making it far easier for the unlicensed station to get grants and tax-deductible contributions. The station's openness generated a lot of publicity, including stories in the *Boston Globe* and even a plug for one of its fundraisers in the *Boston Herald*.[36]

Despite strong community support, the FCC shut down Radio Free Allston, acting upon a complaint filed by the management of WROR, a corporate-owned station, which contended that "the so-called Radio Free Allston is operating too close to us on the dial." Responding to the complaint, FCC agents confronted Radio Free Allston on October 28, shortly after Steve Provizer stepped in as deejay to relieve Pastor Rose Aubourg, whose weekly *Solid Rock"* Bible show ended at 5:00 p.m. The agents ordered Provizer to shut down the station or face a fine and imprisonment. He complied.[37]

The FCC's action generated complaints from community groups and activists. Former City Councilor Dave Scondrus, who had a weekly show on Radio Free Allston, asked state legislators to help. State Representative Byron Rushing announced that he would introduce legislation to help the station. "If there's anything we can do through legislation to allow Radio Free Allston to function in Massachusetts, we'll do it," Rushing said. And the American Civil Liberties Union of Massachusetts offered to represent the free station in its appeal.[38]

FCC officials ridiculed these actions, saying that states cannot oversee FCC actions. "The FCC is authorized by Congress to regulate both interstate and intrastate communication," said Magalie Sales, an FCC spokesperson, rejecting the notion that Massachusetts legislators had any power to help the free station.

In October and November, the FCC sent warning letters to several micropower community stations, including Free Radio Memphis, KAW-FM in Lawrence, Kansas, and Radio Mutiny in Philadelphia.[39] The stations disregarded the FCC warnings and continued broadcasting.

In November the FCC continued its attempts to silence unlicensed stations. On November 19 FCC agents in Tampa, Florida, simultaneously raided Temple Terrace Community Radio (aka the Party Pirate), Radio Free Tampa Bay (aka 87X) and Lutz Community Radio. The raids, although consistent with what the FCC was doing in other parts of the United States, were due in part to Temple Terrace Community Radio founder Doug Brewer's increasingly brazen attitude towards the FCC. Brewer had increased the station's power to 125 watts, making it audible throughout much of Tampa, and it started carrying commercials for small businesses, including used record stores and strip joints. Brewer printed up bumper stickers promoting the station as "Tampa's Party Pirate – 102.1 FM" and T-shirts reading "License? We don't need no stinking license." He also repeatedly engaged in on-air sexual talk, which led the local alternative newspaper, the *Weekly Planet*, to christen him "Best Pig of the Airwaves."

Brewer's activities, rather than alienating listeners, made him and the unlicensed station more popular in Tampa. It also endeared him to the dozens of deejays who volunteered at the station, including Tom Scruggs (aka "Scooter Macgruder") of the Temple Terrace United Methodist Church, who hosted a Christian rock show on Sundays for nearly nine months before the unlicensed station was closed own. "God led me to this show, and if he wants me to continue, in whatever form, I'm ready," said Scruggs about his work at the Party Pirate.[40]

Brewer's activities were such that they were covered in a front page story in the *Wall Street Journal*, in which Brewer challenged the FCC to take action. "It's going, it's visible, and it just plain rocks," said Brewer about The Party Pirate. Ralph Barlow, the district director of the FCC's Tampa field office, responded that Brewer's taunts were "not good" for FCC employee morale. "This guy is going off the deep end," Barlow said, "Sooner or later I'll nail him."[41]

Barlow acted sooner rather than later, ostensibly on a complaint filed by commercial station WHPT-FM. At half past six on the morning of November 19, gun-toting police, FCC agents, and federal marshals pounded on the door of Brewer's home. Brewer awakened, thinking he had heard thunder. When he finally opened the door, Brewer was handcuffed and thrown to the floor. During the next twelve hours, FCC agents disassembled the studio of the unlicensed station, which was located in Brewer's garage, and seized everything that resembled broadcasting equipment.[42]

A few miles away, FCC agents and U.S. marshals raided the homes of Kelly Kombat and Lonnie Kobres, seizing the transmitters of 87X and Lutz Community Radio. Of the three unlicensed broadcasters busted in Tampa that morning, only Kobres was charged with felonies for broadcasting without a license. Federal officials contended that he was charged because he had continued to broadcast after the previous raid, not because of his political viewpoints.[43] "Ninety illegal broadcasters have been shot down in the past year with no more action than sending letters or visiting them and delivering warnings," an FCC official explained about the felony charges. "Still, we do want to get across to the public that this is a serious matter, and what the consequences there are to public safety and to the broadcasters themselves."[44]

The Micropower Movement Responds

News of the FCC raids in Tampa were distributed nationwide almost immediately over the internet to other microradio broadcasters, who encouraged Brewer, Kombat, and Kobres to organize a local movement protesting the FCC's actions. A national committee was also established to raise money for Kobres's defense, which likewise used the internet to distribute information and solicit funds.[45]

In Tampa, supporters of the free stations swamped the FCC and WHPT-FM with protest calls. The calls were so frequent that the FCC and WHPT stopped answering their phones, and WHPT general manager Drew Rashbaum refused to comment about his station's complaint because of the harassment it had received from "obnoxious listeners" of the unlicensed station, as he referred to them.[46]

Protest demonstrations against the FCC raids were organized in Tampa. On Tuesday, November 25, over 100 supporters of the free radio stations gathered in front of the FCC's Tampa office. "They're not going to get rid of us," declared Party Pirate deejay Matthew Adelman, one of the many dozens of protesters who assembled at the federal office with placards reading, "Federal Censorship Commission" and "What Good is Free Speech if You Can't Hear Us?" "They're going to have to deal with us," Adelman said.

In the midst of the protests, where Brewer and Kombat addressed their supporters, 102.1 FM defiantly returned to the air from an undisclosed location, playing the Ramones song, "We Want the Airwaves." A cellular phone linked to the station was passed around and protesters voiced their disapproval of the FCC,

sometimes profanely, and their comments were broadcast by the unlicensed station. "I don't have anything to do with it," said Brewer about the broadcasts. "My
disk jockeys, they're crazy kinds of guys."[47]

Rather than returning to the air, Brewer created an internet-based broadcast
that has become increasingly offensive and irresponsible. Brewer's internet broadcasts have included assertions that the U.S. government is run by Communists,
pictures of scantily clad women, and even an interview with former Ku Klux Klan
grand wizard David Duke.[48]

Rather than deterring free radio broadcasters, the FCC's actions actually
strengthened the resolve of many to remain on the air. Free Radio Memphis,
Radio Mutiny, and KAW-FM vowed to fight on, and several microradio stations
that had previously signed off in the face of FCC pressures returned to the air.
Radio Mutiny activists vowed to put ten free stations on the air for every one that
the FCC shut down. In Austin, Texas, a conservative Christian station on 88.5 FM
resumed broadcasting, and in Milwaukee, WTPS reoccupied 99.9 FM. In
Michigan, Pastor Rick Strawcutter returned to the air after a four-and-a-half-
month hiatus.[49]

In Philadelphia, supporters of Radio Mutiny also protested the FCC's actions.
On December 1, thirty people staged a demonstration against the FCC's letter ordering the station off the air. The protest, like the one in Tampa, featured a live
broadcast, where protesters voiced their opinions about the FCC and NAB over
the airwaves. "We are going to fight this in the courts and streets," said Paul Davis,
a Radio Mutiny supporter.[50]

Microradio supporters took other actions to frustrate the FCC. Radio Mutiny
organized a tour of the eastern states to promote community microradio, demonstrating how easy it is to operate a free radio station. In Tennessee, Mutiny activist
Pete Tridish helped Black Liberation Radio in Chattanooga get off the ground.
And in Boston, supporters of Radio Free Allston filed petitions opposing the license renewal of WROR, the station that urged the FCC to shut down the unlicensed community station.

Despite these actions, the FCC continued its assault on free radio, much to the
delight of the NAB. On December 9, FCC agents visited the Old Firehouse Cafe in
Anchorage, Alaska, from where Free Radio Spenard broadcast. The agents said
they would return and confiscate the equipment if the station were not shut
down. "We turned it off Tuesday night after having a meeting," said a Free Radio
Spenard volunteer. The transmitter was disassembled and hidden.[51]

In January 1998 the NAB's Radio Board met, and a report on unlicensed broadcasting was presented by Executive Vice President Jeff Baumann. Baumann
proudly announced that the FCC had shut down nearly 100 unlicensed stations in
1997.[52] The Board passed another resolution supporting the FCC's silencing of
free radio broadcasters.

The free radio movement responded with its own meetings, including one in
New York in February, another in Philadelphia in early April, and one in Las

Vegas, designed to coincide with the NAB's annual convention there in mid-April. The New York gathering was billed as a Micropower Radio Benefit, sponsored by the New York Free Media Alliance, Steal This Radio, and Philadelphia's Radio Mutiny. The New York gathering included a dance, a fundraiser to help pay for the upcoming Philadelphia conference, and workshops held in different parts of the city. Workshops in East Harlem and the South Bronx taught by New York City and Philadelphia free radio activists attracted forty people, who were shown how to start their own free stations. As a result of the workshops, four more free stations were started in New York City.[53]

The Philadelphia and Las Vegas conference included sessions on technical and legal issues for microradio broadcasters and how-to workshops for local community organizers, who were given instruction on how to start microradio stations. The Las Vegas conference included a protest directed at the NAB and corporate control of the airwaves.[54]

Although the demonstrations did garner some newspaper and magazine coverage, including an article in *Time* magazine that described the Las Vegas protest as "an oddly surreal, 60s-style pageant," they did not slow the FCC's assault on the microradio movement. During the first quarter of 1998, the FCC shut down sixty-seven stations, but many of these returned to the air. In San Marcos and Leander, Texas, Chewellah and Oroville, Washington, and Cleveland, Ohio, the FCC sought from administrative law judges cease-and-desist orders against microstation operators who continued broadcasting after being warned by the FCC to stop.[55]

Moreover, under pressure from the FCC, the NAB, and the federal court decisions in Minnesota and Florida, Judge Claudia Wilken finally sided with the FCC and issued a permanent injunction against Stephen Dunifer and Free Radio Berkeley on June 16, 1998. The injunction was issued on narrow procedural grounds rather than constitutional grounds; Wilken ruled that Dunifer's challenge to the constitutionality of FCC regulations did not have standing because he never applied to the commission for a license. Wilken enjoined "Dunifer, and all persons in active concert or participation with him . . . from making radio transmissions in the United States until they first obtain a license from the FCC."[56] "This isn't the end," said attorney Luke Hiken, who said he would file a motion with Judge Wilken to reconsider her ruling. "This is a case that could drag on for fifty years."[57]

As a result of the court decision, Free Radio Berkeley's aboveground broadcasts ceased on June 17. As the station was being closed, Dunifer said that "rumor has it that other folks if necessary will return to the Sunday night broadcasts from the hills, like we used to do."[58]

The FCC Reconsiders Its Strategy

When the FCC began its campaign against free radio, the Commission itself was bitterly divided. The chair of the FCC, Reed E. Hundt, was engaged in a bitter feud over children's programming policy with several commissioners, including Andrew C. Barrett and James Quello, who were close allies of the commercial broadcasting industry. Quello, first appointed to the FCC by President Nixon in 1974, was not only a former broadcaster, but functioned as the broadcast industry's emissary to the Commission, ensuring that the agency served the interests of media corporations rather than the public. Quello opposed rules requiring television stations to carry educational programming for children, favored loosening rules on broadcast station ownership, and had even campaigned for the elimination of the Fairness Doctrine. The disputes were so bitter that Hundt, Barrett, and Quello announced that they would not be returning to the FCC.[59]

By fall 1997, when the FCC's nastiest assault on unlicensed broadcasting began, the U.S. Senate was in the midst of confirming four new commissioners, replacing those who were leaving. Two were Democrats and two were Republicans. Stepping in as new FCC chair was William E. Kennard, the FCC's general counsel and a former assistant general counsel for the NAB, who was confirmed in a ninety-nine to one vote on October 29, 1997.[60] Kennard's near-unanimous vote indicated that he had the support of industry lobbyists, including the NAB. In fact, after joining the FCC Kennard had attended NAB conventions in Las Vegas, including the 1997 convention where FCC Compliance and Information Bureau Chief Beverly Baker doled out advice to commercial broadcasters on how they could help silence unlicensed stations. At that conference, Kennard described to NAB members the "arsenal" of weapons the Commission might use against free radio stations.[61]

Kennard was appointed chair of the FCC not just because of his experience at the agency and support from industry groups, but because of "his open mind" and "his willingness to compromise," the *New York Times* reported.[62] Kennard's reputation as a compromiser did not mean that he would abandon the policy pursued by the FCC since its inception—promoting commercial broadcasting at the expense of community broadcasting. Rather it meant that he would try to find a way to accommodate dissenting views, particularly when the dissenting views captured public attention, as the views of microbroadcasters were doing in the wake of the FCC's campaign against microbroadcasting. Across the country, newspapers—even those co-owned by radio stations—were describing the FCC's campaign as overzealous.

When asked by the *New York Times* in December about his attitude toward the free radio movement for an article about Free Radio Berkeley, Kennard said that unlicensed stations constitute "a terrible safety problem. . . . We just can't allow a situation where you have illegal broadcasters disrupting communications between pilots and control towers." However, he added that "I am personally very concerned that we have more outlets for expressions over the airwaves. I have made it a point of my tenure here as chairman to try to spotlight the fact that the broadcast industry is consolidating at a very rapid pace. And as a result of this, there are fewer opportunities of entry to minority groups, community groups, small businesses in general. And I'm very interested in hearing ideas to remedy the unfortunate closing of opportunities for a lot of new entrants."[63]

Kennard's public pronouncement about his willingness to examine "ideas to remedy" the lack of public access to the airwaves drew a quick response from the free radio movement. The Association of Micropower Broadcasters issued an open letter to Kennard congratulating him on his "promotion to chairman of the FCC" and his "fresh [ideas] for heading up the agency." The letter proposed that the agency "create a micropower fm band between 88 and 92 megahertz," that the band have "a minimal filing fee so people of limited means can also gain access to the airwaves," and that limits be placed on the number of stations that "can be owned by a single company in a community." Over the internet, the micropower movement organized a letter-writing and e-mail campaign directed at Kennard, pressuring him to change FCC policies.[64] Newspaper reports about the FCC's campaign against free radio broadcasters continued to be published, often carrying quotes from unlicensed broadcasters that were embarrassing to the FCC. For example, the *Florida Times-Union* of Jacksonville published a story about the FCC's crackdown on unlicensed stations that quoted Doug Brewer, who described his arrest. "It was a surprise attack. They came in with a real vengeance," he reported. "If I were a drug dealer or a murderer, that would be different story. All I had was a radio transmitter. I wasn't hurting anybody."[65]

The pressure and continuing publicity caused the FCC in February 1998 to dust off a petition to establish a microradio broadcasting system, a petition that had been sitting in its files for six months.[66] The petition requested that the FCC assign "one AM broadcast and one FM broadcast channel to [a] microstation radio broadcasting service. The channels would be shared by the licensed microstations." The petition also suggested that the stations operate with a measly one watt of power, making them inaudible to anyone not very near the transmitter.[67] Rather than calling for comments on the petition, the FCC decided to hold an inquiry on *whether* it should hold an inquiry.

The petition that the FCC put on the table was as conservative as possible. It proposed that microbroadcasters be assigned just one frequency in each broadcasting band and that high schools and universities, not community groups, be given priority in the licensing process. Moreover, the proposal suggested that microstations be commercial, providing access for "entrepreneurs" who are "motivated by the prospect of genuine wealth." Thus, the petition never addressed any of the inequities against which the microradio movement was rebelling.[68]

Despite the conservatism of the microradio station proposal, the NAB quickly pronounced its opposition to any and all microradio broadcasting. NAB president Edward Fritts said, "At a time when spectrum used for radio stations is overly congested, it would be folly to authorize hundreds of additional low-power stations that would surely cause additional interference." Other representatives of commercial broadcasting also spoke out against microradio broadcasting, confirming what had been believed by most microradio broadcasters all along—that commercial broadcasters were not opposed to free stations because they operated without licenses, but because the free stations represented competition.[69] Free stations attract listeners who are disenchanted with commercial radio programming, demonstrate that commercial stations fail to serve the public interest, and represent an alternative to corporate station ownership. Thus, microradio stations, regardless of whether they are legal or illegal, threaten the very raison d'etre of the U.S. system of corporate broadcasting.

The Future of Microradio

If the FCC functions during the inquiry into establishing a microradio system as it did during its efforts to silence Free Radio Berkeley—misrepresenting facts, failing to act in a timely manner, and exaggerating the interference caused by the station—the inquiry could become more of a public relations campaign to deflect criticism of its policies than an effort to actually change policy. The FCC, in effect, could use the inquiry to buy time and goodwill, as it figures out what to do next about unlicensed broadcasters.

There is some evidence that the inquiry is a public relations effort. In a letter to *USA Today*, Kennard criticized a story about free radio broadcasting for "glamorizing so-called pirate radio broadcasters as 'good guys.'" As evidence that FCC officials, not free radio broadcasters, are the "good guys," Kennard cited the inquiry. He wrote, "Of particular relevance here, the FCC asked for public comment on a petition asking the FCC to begin a rulemaking to license a one-watt community-based low-power radio service." However, Kennard repeated the corporation-manufactured canard that "unlicensed low-power stations interfere with programming from licensed stations" and "air traffic control communications." He also asserted that the claim that FCC "policies are designed only to benefit 'rich corporations' is false," thereby justifying the FCC's policy of raiding and closing free radio stations. "The FCC will not condone illegal broadcasting," he wrote.[70]

In fact, the FCC continued its attempts to silence free radio stations. On March 5, 1998, FCC agents visited Steal This Radio and threatened to return with U.S. marshals if the station did not go off the air. To avoid a raid, the station temporarily signed off.[71]

This suggests that the FCC is engaged in a public relations campaign. If it is a public campaign, the micropower radio inquiry will die a slow death. The FCC often acts as though inaction is the best remedy to problems, as shown by its initial responses to Free Radio Berkeley and the growth of free radio. In the Free Radio Berkeley case, they ignored Stephen Dunifer's appeal of its forfeiture notice, hoping that the situation could be remedied in another venue—in court. During this time, the micropower radio movement grew, rather than died, as the FCC had hoped would happen. The same will occur this time. If the FCC drags its feet rather than legalizes low-power community radio stations, the number of free radio stations will continue to grow. This is what occurred in Belgium and

France, despite repressive acts by government authorities. As events in these countries show, raiding stations, arresting their operators, and seizing transmitters is not an effective method for restoring order on the airwaves. Once citizens are able to speak into a microphone, they will not be satisfied with prehistoric modes of communication again. This attitude was exemplified by the protesters in Tampa, who carried placards reading, "What Good is Free Speech if You Can't Hear Us?" There, despite the raids and arrests, free radio stations have remained on the air.

If the FCC's intent is to stall for time, hoping that it can eliminate the "problem" of unlicensed broadcasting during this period rather than providing citizens with access to the airwaves, it may increase the penalties for unlicensed broadcasting, as was done in Taiwan. Governments, including the U.S. government, often resort to increasing penalties to force compliance with their rules and laws. History is replete with examples of this.

There is also some evidence that the FCC is pursuing a more repressive strategy with microbroadcasters. In Tampa, the FCC's raid on Doug Brewers's home was far more militant than previous raids. And in Tampa, Lonnie Kobres was charged with felonies for operating Lutz Community Radio. This was the first time that an individual was charged with felonies for merely broadcasting without a license.[72] The FCC could pursue felony charges against other free radio broadcasters in an effort to repress the movement.

The FCC could also adopt an anemic rule permitting low-power radio, such as the one it put on the table in February 1998. This proposal does not challenge corporate control of the airwaves, provides communities with just one AM and FM low-power frequency, and limits the power of community stations to one-watt, far less than the power of most currently operating, unlicensed micropower stations. By adopting a policy such as this, the FCC could pretend that it is providing citizens access to the airwaves, when indeed it is not. One frequency per band is too few to provide real programming diversity , and one watt of power is so little that it is equivalent to handing community groups a bullhorn rather than a transmitter.

Given the FCC's past history, it is likely to adopt a policy that does not in any way alter the existing patterns of station ownership. While the NAB has voiced opposition to all low-power broadcasting, it could easily live with one-watt stations operating on a single frequency, because these would too weak and too few in number to be influential.

If the FCC does adopt an anemic policy, some free stations might apply for licenses and reduce their powers of operation, but most won't. Once community groups have been able to speak to 4,000 people with 40 watts of power, its unlikely that they will be willing to speak to just 100 with one watt of power. Once the 40-watt transmitters have been removed from their boxes and assembled, it will be very difficult to disassemble them and get them back in. This is true not only in the United States, but the rest of the world as well.

Thus, the U.S. will likely see the free radio war continue if the FCC adopts another policy that inhibits the development of community radio. A war of this type would undoubtedly escalate, with the FCC adopting harsher and harsher penalties for unlicensed broadcasting.

History shows that there is no substitute for a real community broadcasting system of the type adopted in Belgium after the free radio movement there. A community broadcasting system should be based on stations operating at less than 100 watts, but at far more than one or two watts. A community broadcasting system requires multiple frequencies in each city, not just one or two. The FCC could easily create such a system by designating existing translator frequencies for this purpose. Translators stations are currently permitted to broadcast with fewer than 100 watts, but do not originate programming. Instead, translator stations merely relay the signal of another, higher-power licensed station.

It is unlikely that the FCC will change its translator policy because most translator frequencies are already occupied by commercial broadcasters. In fact, the FCC explicitly rejected this proposal previously at the urging of commercial broadcasters, who represent a powerful lobbying group in Washington. Commercial broadcasters provide donations to Democratic and Republican candidates for federal office, and they wine and dine FCC officials at events such as the NAB convention in Las Vegas. In addition, they reward retiring FCC officials with high-paying jobs when the officials leave government.

Ultimately, the only way to alter the current system is to curb the power that corporations now wield over government. Steps to curb corporate power include banning contributions from *corporate* political action committees (PACs), which now constitute the vast majority of PAC money flowing into political campaigns, and reversing court decisions that have given corporations rights as individuals.

Ultimately, the only way to adopt such legislation is by building grassroots community organizations—such as the Green Party, Public Citizen, and Democracy Unlimited—that do not depend upon or even accept corporate monies, which have strings attached. It is no accident that groups such as the Green Party have supported the free radio movement.[73] These groups realize that free radio is one of the few avenues available to individual citizens and community groups who wish to speak against the excesses of corporate capitalism. As other grassroots groups discover free radio, they will undoubtedly also embrace the movement. When they do, the system will be forced to change, just as it did in France when groups such as the Socialist party finally embraced free radio.

NOTES

1. Lawrence C. Soley and John S. Nichols, *Clandestine Radio Broadcasting* (New York: Praeger, 1987), p. 251.

2. "Colombia: Update on Peace Negotiations and Related Developments," *Notisur* (Publication of the Latin America Institute at the University of New Mexico), June 30,

1992; Reuters, "More than 50 Servicemen, Guerrillas Killed in Colombian Battle," December 12, 1990, BC cycle.

3. "Burma Can't Silence Radio Voices of Democracy," *Chicago Tribune,* January 4, 1998, p. 12.

4. British Broadcasting Corporation, "Papua New Guinea Protests Over Australian Assistance to Rebel Radio," *BBC Summary of World Broadcasts,* February 3, 1992, p. 1294.

5. "Minister, Envoy Discuss Clandestine Radio Station," *Foreign Broadcast Information Service,* July 13, 1992, p. 6; "Massacres Spreading in Rwanda," *New York Times,* April 19, 1994, p. A3.

6. "Taiwan: Pirate Broadcasters Cling to Airwaves," *International Freedom of Expression Exchange Communiqué #6–47,* December 2, 1997. On-line posting, available from <http://www.ifex.org>.

7. *United States Telephone Association v. FCC,* 28 F. 3rd 1232 (DC Cir. 1994).

8. "Memorandum and Order Denying Plaintiff's Motion for Preliminary Injunction and Staying Action," *United States v. Stephen Paul Dunifer,* No. C 94–03542 CW (January 30, 1995). See also "Response to the Notice of Apparent Liability" by Louis N. Hiken, addressed to Philip M. Kane, Acting Engineer in Charge, FCC, Hayward, Calif., June 28, 1993, pp. 3–4.

9. "Report and Order 97–218," 8 *Comm. Reg.* (P & F) 1314 (June 28, 1997).

10. Jack Goodman, Broadcast Engineering Conference session on "Radio: Technical-Regulatory Issues," National Association of Broadcasters 1997 Annual Conference, Las Vegas, April 5–10, 1997.

11. Ibid.

12. Ibid.

13. For example, see FCC Audio Services Division, "Low Power Broadcast Radio Station," April 1996, on-line posting, available from: <http://www.fcc.gov/asd/lowpower.html#PROHIBITED>, November 19, 1997.

14. David Sommer, "Lutz Radio Station Equipment Seized," *Tampa Tribune,* March 9, 1996, p. 1.

15. Jahi Kubweza, telephone interview by author, January 2, 1996.

16. Simon Peter Groebner, "Pirate Radio Wavemaking," *Minneapolis City Pages,* September 23, 1996, on-line posting, available from: <http://citypages.com/thepaper/detail.asp?/ArticlesID=3201>.

17. Ibid. For a discussion of other conflicts involving The Beat, see Brian Lambert, "Officials Plunder Pirate Radio Station's Equipment," *St. Paul Pioneer Press,* November 2, 1996, p. 1E.

18. FCC Compliance and Information Bureau, Tampa Field Office, "Pirate Stations Beware: FCC Shuts Down Pirate Station in Orlando, Florida," December 11, 1996.

19. Beverly Baker, panel discussion on "Radio: Technical-Regulatory Issues," Broadcast Engineering Conference, National Association of Broadcasters 1997 Annual Conference, Las Vegas, April 5–10, 1997.

20. Ibid.

21. Paige Albiniak, "Low Power to the People," *Broadcasting and Cable,* September 8, 1997, p. 22.

22. Bill Stevens, "Greetings Teeming Millions!" *WTPS Newsletter,* June 1997.

23. "Statement of NAB President and CEO Edward O. Fritts on Recent Actions Resulting in shutdown of Pirate Stations in New Jersey and Florida," Release S23/97, September 5, 1997, on-line posting, available from: <http://www.nab.org/statements/ s2397.html>; Jim Hana, "FCC Turns Off Radio Pirates," *In These Times*, February 8, 1998, p. 7; Matt Spangler, "FCC Tries to Sink Pirate Operations," *Radio & Records*, November 7, 1997, p. 15.

24. The FCC was apparently aware several days in advance that it was about to win the case against Kobres. Agents were sent on August 22 to the apartment of Jim Pierrilus, who operated an unlicensed station on 89.9 FM in Fort Walton Beach, Florida. The agents warned Pierrilus that he could be fined $11,000 for operating an unlicensed station and then asked him to voluntarily hand over the transmitter, which he did. See "FCC Shuts Down Unlicensed Radio Operation in Fort Walton Beach, FL," August 22, 1997 (Report No. CI 97–7), on-line posting, available from: <http://www.fcc.gov/cib/ News_Releases/ nrci7011.html>.

25. "FCC Wins Summary Judgment Against Unlicensed Radio Operator," September 12, 1997 (NEWSReport No. CI 97–9); "FCC Wins Court Action Against Unlicensed Radio Operator," September 10, 1997 (NEWSReport No. CI 97–8), on-line postings, available from: <http://www.fcc.gov/Bureaus/Compliance/ News_Releases/1997/rci7012.txt>.

26. Dennis Wharton and John Earnhardt, "NAB To Pirate Broadcasters: Illegal Is Illegal," press release, February 2, 1998, on-line posting, available from: <http://www.nab.org/PressRel/Releases/0298>. The press release included a law-and-order statement by NAB president Edward O. Fritts, who said, "Pirate radio broadcasters are illegal. Period. The court should affirm the rights of legal broadcasters, but should not tolerate or condone lawbreakers."

27. Vincent Kajunski, the FCC's deputy director for New England, reports that the commission adopted a new set of priorities regarding unlicensed stations, but other FCC officials have denied this. See Jesse Walker, "Rebel Radio," *New Republic*, March 9, 1998, p. 11.

28. Harriet Ryan, "Station Silenced as Pirate," *Asbury Park Press*, September 5, 1997, p. A1; "FCC Officials and Federal Marshals Raided an Unlicensed Radio Station," *Broadcasting*, September 8, 1997.

29. "FCC Closes Down Unlicensed Radio Operator," September 25, 1995, on-line posting, available from: <http://www.fcc.gov/cib/News_Releases/nrci/7015.html>.

30. Mark Larson, "Radio Station Shut Down by Feds Set to Start Again," *Business Journal – Sacramento*, October 10, 1997, p. 10.

31. Robert D. Davila, "Owner Says FCC Seizure of Equipment Won't Quiet Radio Station," *Sacramento Bee*, September 27, 1997, p. B5; J. Nils Wright, "Low Watts Spark Big Row," *Business Journal – Sacramento*, October 21, 1996, p. 1.

32. "FCC Crosses Swords with Pirate Radio DJ," *Florida Times Union*, December 29, 1997, p. A6; Tom Perrin, "Radio Station Fighting for the Airwaves," *Kansas City Star*, November 13, 1997, p. A1.

33. Joseph Mont, "Radio Pirate Draws Diverse Following," *The Cambridge TAB*, January 14–20, 1997, pp. 15–16.

34. Daniel Gewertz, "Rockin' the (Banana) Boat," *Boston Herald*, May 22, 1997, pp. 52–53.

35. Lynn Meadows, "FCC vs. Pirates: No Solution Soon," *Radio World*, February 18, 1998, p. 10.

36. Gewertz, "Rockin' the (Banana) Boat"; Susan Bickelhaupt, "Unlicensed, Anti-Format Radio Free Allston," *Boston Globe,* August 14, 1997, p. E8.

37. Cate McQuaid, "FCC Forces Radio Free Allston Off Air," *Boston Globe,* November 2, 1997, p. 10.

38. Ibid.

39. Jim Hanas, "FCC Turns Off Radio Pirates, *In These Times,* February 8, 1998, p. 7; Tom Perrin, "Radio Station Fighting for Airwaves," *Kansas City Star,* November 13, 1997, p. A1.

40. Michelle Bearden, "Pirate Radio Was Ministry," *Tampa Tribune,* November 29, 1997, p. 4.

41. Bruce Orwall, "Mr. Brewer the Pirate Doesn't Rule the Waves, He Just Makes Them," *Wall Street Journal,* October 21, 1997, pp. A1, A15.

42. Richard Danielson, "Marshals Take Out Pirate Radio," *St. Petersburg Times,* November 20, 1997, p. 1A; Alexander Cockburn, "Free Radio, Crazy Cops and Broken Windows," *Nation,* December 15, 1997, p. 9.

43. However, the officials did point out that Kobres and his wife, Cheryl, were unindicted coconspirators in a case involving a "Constitutional Common Law Court" operated by a militia group. See Dean Solov, "Feds Shut Down Pirate Radio Stations," *Tampa Tribune,* November 20, 1997, p. 1.

44. Mary Curtius, "Defiant Pirates Ply the Airwaves," *Los Angeles Times,* March 5, 1998, p. A20.

45. "Support Lonnie Kobres' Defense," January 16, 1998, on-line posting, discussion list, available from: Grassroots News Network, <GRASSROOTS@tao.com>; also available from: <RADIO@tao.ca>.

46. Richard Danielson, "Radio Pirates in Escalating War with Rules," *St. Petersburg Times,* November 28, 1997, p. 1B.

47. Dean Solov, "Pirate Radio Supporters Reclaim Spot on the Dial," *Tampa Tribune,* November 26, 1997, p. 10.

48. Dean Solov, "Phantom Powers 'Pirate' on the Air," *Tampa Tribune,* February 10, 1998, p. 5; Kelly Kombat, telephone interview by author, December 1, 1997; American Dissident Voices, on-line posting, available from: <http://www.natvan.com/internet-radio>, March 30, 1998.

49. Rob Patterson, "Pirate Radio Still Afloat," *Austin American-Statesman,* January 22, 1998, p. 19; "Strawcutter Returns to the Air," *AMPB Report* (A Publication of the Association for Micropower Broadcasters) 22.

50. Yvonne Latty, "Mutiny on the Airwaves," *Philadelphia Daily News,* December 2, 1997, p. 12.

51. Mike Dunham, "'Free Radio Spenard' Pulls Plug After FCC Visit," *Anchorage Daily News,* December 11, 1997, p. 2D.

52. Lynn Meadows, "FCC vs. Pirates: No Solution Soon," *Radio World,* February 18, 1998.

53. Greg Ruggiero, e-mail to author, February 25, 1998.

54. "Liberating the Airwaves—Events and Strategies," *AMPB Report* (A Publication of the Association for Micropower Broadcasters) 22.

55. Margaret Hornblower, "Radio Free America," *Time,* April 20, 1996, p. 4; Leslie Stimson, "Low-power Protestors Shadow Radio Debate," *Radio World,* April 29, 1998, p. 9.

56. Charles Burress, "FCC Wins License Battle with Free Radio Berkeley," *San Francisco Chronicle,* June 18, 1998, p. A27; "Rebel Broadcasters Lose Legal Battle," *Sacramento Bee,*

June 17, 1998, p. A4; "FCC Defeats Berkeley Radio Pirate," *Communications Daily*, June 18, 1998, p. 1.

57. Louis Hiken, telephone interview by author, June 23, 1998.

58. Burress, "FCC Wins License Battle with Free Radio Berkeley."

59. "Longtime F.C.C. Member Plans to Retire," *New York Times*, January 2, 1997, p. C31; Edmund Andrews, "A Bitter Feud Fouls Lines at the F.C.C.," *New York Times*, November 20, 1995, p. D1.

60. "Senate Approves New F.C.C. Chairman," *New York Times*, October 30, 1997, p. D12.

61. "NAB Notebook," *Television Digest*, April 14, 1997.

62. Seth Schiesel, "All Too Soon, New F.C.C. Chief Finds Welcome Is Cooling," *New York Times*, March 23, 1998, p. D1.

63. Julie Lew, "Radio's Renegade," *New York Times*, December 8, 1997, p. D12.

64. "An Open Letter to William Kennard," *AMPB Report* (A Publication of the Association of Micropower Broadcasters) 22.

65. "FCC Crosses Swords with Pirate Radio Djs," *Florida Time-Union*, December 29, 1997, p. A6.

66. "Petition for Micropower Radio Broadcasting Service," February 5, 1998, on-line posting, available from: <http://fcc.gov/mmb/asd/lowpwr.html>.

67. "Before the Federal Communication Commission: Petition for a Microstation Radio Broadcasting Service" submitted by Nickolaus Legget, Judith Legget, and Donald Schellhardt, June 26, 1997.

68. Ibid.

69. Chris McConnell, "FCC Considers Low-Power Radio," *Broadcasting & Cable*, March 9, 1998, p. 19.

70. William Kennard, "Radio 'Pirates' Interfere, Break Law, Create Safety Hazards," *USA Today*, March 9, 1998, p. 18A.

71. Greg Ruggiero, letter to author, March 23, 1998; Greg Ruggiero, telephone interview by author, March 31, 1998.

72. It was also the first time someone was convicted of felonies for merely operating an unlicensed station. On February 22, Kobres was convicted of fourteen felonies for broadcasting without a license and, as a result, is facing twenty-eight years in prison and a $3.8 million fine. Kobres's attorney, Larry Becraft, best known as a defender of tax protesters, unsuccessfully argued that the FCC's mandate to control the airwaves was not legal because it was not published in the *Federal Register*. When the judge ruled against this defense, Kobres was forced to argue that he was unaware of the rules, which the jury didn't buy. See Bill Coats, "'Pirate Radio' Debate to Air at Hillsborough Trial," *St. Petersburg Times*, February 23, 1998, p. 3B; Bill Coats, "Jury Convicts Lutz Radio Broadcasters," *St. Petersburg Times*, February 26, 1998, p. 4B.

73. For example, the Green Party at its 1996 convention in Los Angeles endorsed the free radio movement and even featured a workshop on how to operate a free radio station. At that convention, the Green Party nominated Public Citizen leader Ralph Nader as its presidential candidate. In Milwaukee, the Greens organization filed a petition with the FCC opposing Saga Communication Corporation's request to put a translator station 99.9 FM, the frequency on which the unlicensed WTPS operated. See "Application for Construction Permit for a New FM Translator," FCC file BPFT–961004TB.

Index